What Pe(ople are saying about)
Re-(becca) and Me
Life Now with My Little 2-Letter Friend

Beyond words … as she danced through her life story … situation after situation with the trials and tribulations that only God could re-enable one's path from Lost to Found … you'll be touched beyond belief … a MUST read!

Dr. Bob Ward, author of *Building the Perfect Star* and *Sports Speed*, Sports Scientist and former Dallas Cowboys Strength & Conditioning Coach (1976–89)

There is so much strength when survivors stand and tell their stories, which Rebecca does here so beautifully. In her own words, this compelling story is truly powerful and transformative. You'll be inspired by her tenacity and courage as she breaks through the shroud of darkness and finds hope, healing, and renewal.

Courtney Underwood, Survivor Namesake, Courtney's SAFE Place at The Turning Point Rape Crisis Center, Owner & CEO, Underwood Commercial Properties

I found this to be an intriguing and fascinating read that I could hardly put down. As a licensed professional family therapist who has specialized in the field of sexual offense for the past 25 years, I can say that Rebecca accurately describes the difficult circumstances accompanied by the deep emotions victims of sexual violence commonly experience. What makes Rebecca's story unique is that she brings a strong message of hope to others that healing and wholeness are possible … for survivors as well as offenders.

Anna Shursen, PhD.

Eye opening account of every woman's worst nightmare. Follow Rebecca's journey from struggle after struggle to the point where her life takes on new and everlasting meaning. Every victim of sexual assault, police officer, physician, and counselor can benefit from the accounts recorded by Rebecca.

John Ritchie, Chief of Police Retired, Alexandria, Louisiana

Told with suspense and marvelous word images, it is a great story of someone seeking the best ... with the guts to challenge life and its limitations. There is a real message here for women, or anyone, going through a life-changing experience ... and how to survive with self-worth and faith intact.

> Joyce Ward, Dance and Theater Educator, Bally Health Club-DFW, former Aerobic Fitness Creator/Director

Are you looking for absolute peace? Are you searching for a better understanding of how and when God is working in your life? Well, all answers and more can be found in *Re-and Me*. Rebecca's story is so inspiring and relevant for every reader. It speaks to the reader who has experienced her plight as well as to the reader who just wants to know, or who is looking for, an inspiring true story. I cried; I got mad; I felt compassion, and I felt forgiveness through the eyes of one who had the courage to surrender her will to the Lordship of Christ. Once I started reading, I couldn't stop!

> Rev. Arthur Hallett, National Director of Evangelism Explosion Prison Ministry

Re- *and* Me

Life Now With My Little 2-Letter Friend

REBECCA SWIECZKOWSKI

Re-and Me: Life Now with My Little 2-Letter Friend
Published by: Centered Publishing
Frisco, TX
www.CenteredPublishing.com

This book recounts events in the life of the author according to the author's recollection and from the author's perspective. Dialogue, names, dates, places, events, and details may have been altered for privacy purposes or literary effect.

© 2021 Rebecca Swieczkowski. All rights reserved.

No part of this book may be reproduced in any form or by any mechanical means, including information storage and retrieval systems without permission in writing from the publisher/author, except by a reviewer who may quote passages in a review.

Scripture quotations taken from the *New American Standard Bible**(NASB). © The Lockman Foundation 1960, 1962, 1963, 1968, 1971, 1972, 1973, 1975, 1977, 1995 by the Lockman Foundation.

Used by permission. www.Lockman.org.

Some content taken from *Through Gates of Splendor* by Elisabeth Elliot. © 1981. Used by permission of Tyndale House Publishers. All rights reserved.

Some content taken from *My Utmost for His Highest* by Oswald Chambers, Edited by James Reimann, © 1992 by Oswald Chambers Publications Assn., Ltd. Used by permission of Our Daily Bread Publishing, Grand Rapids MI 49501. All rights reserved.

ISBN 978-0578-93625-3
RELIGION / Christian Living / Personal Memoirs

Front Cover Illustration by Lindsay Carole Swieczkowski
Cover Design by Victoria Wolf, wolfdesignandmarketing.com

All rights reserved by Rebecca Swieczkowski and Centered Publishing.
Printed in the United States of America

CENTERED Publishing

In Loving Memory of Dr. Bob Ward
(July 4, 1933-June 28, 2021)

I also dedicate this book to my business mentor and friend, Dr. Bob Ward, who unexpectedly was called home to be with his Lord a few days before his 88th birthday. He was one of the most superb human beings created by God, a role model and coach to thousands, but to his own family; a godly, humble, and loving husband, father, grandfather, and great grandfather!

I cannot say enough about him and the profoundly positive impact he has had on my life. Again, I am grateful for God's Grace for bringing him into my life.

Contents

Special Thanks xi

Dedication xiii

Foreword xv

Introduction 1

Chapter 1: The Call 5

Chapter 2: The Dallas Cowboys Connection 13

Chapter 3: It's Fun To Stay At The YWCA! 21

Chapter 4: F.U.N. Fitness Systems 27

Chapter 5: The Voice 35

Chapter 6: Are You There? 45

Chapter 7: The Doctors 59

Chapter 8: A Quiet Place 73

Chapter 9: The Profiler 91

Chapter 10: TGIFriday 105

Chapter 11: The Question 115

Chapter 12: All Men Are Jerks! 123

Chapter 13: The Strangest Request 131

Chapter 14: The Key 145

Chapter 15: My Perfect Five-Minute Testimony 157

Chapter 16: The Birth of Re-Becky 173

Chapter 17: The Refiner 187

Chapter 18: Faith*Hope*Love 193

Chapter 19: A Woman's Sacred Place 199

Chapter 20: Trauma—Drama 209

Chapter 21: The Miraculous Call 219

Acknowledgments 233

About the Author 235

Endnotes 239

Special Thanks

A MOST SPECIAL thanks to ALL the "Steel Magnolias" in my life. These are women of influence who have modeled to me the rare blend of non-compromising steely strength of character surrounded by the soft petals of empathy, understanding, and extravagant compassion. I salute you. I admire you. When I grow up, I want to be like you!

- My mother, Mae Beth Morgan Burnett—you left the earth when I was 23, but your love and example have never left my heart.
- My grandmother, Almarine (Mom-Mom) Morgan—the legacy of FAITH.
- My grandmother, Delphia (Mamoo) Burnett—the gift/curse of stubborn determination.
- Jan Pierce—my crazy, charismatic dancer friend who owned "the couch in Conroe"!

Re- *and* Me

- Joyce Ward, my mentor—the successful woman who introduced me to GRACE.
- Sandy Vincent, pastor's wife—practical wisdom, keen insight, and perseverance.
- Phyllis Word, my matron of honor—a beautifully humble friend who exemplifies serving with joy.
- Denise Van Bibber & Ms. Ann Masden, my original Steel Magnolias—always elevating the young women around them and inspiring others to pursue God's unique purpose for them.
- Colleen Bien, my forever friend—godmother to Joffrey and mother extraordinaire to her four boys!
- Maggie Amrhein, my New Yorker/Florida Pilates mentor—an incredible open heart and open home.
- Lesley Snelson, faithful friend—Sr. Pilates trainer, creative genius, activist for women's issues.
- Kerri, my sister in the Lord—cancer widow, advocate for grieving children, and workout partner.

Dedication

I DEDICATE THIS book to my wonderful husband, Michael, and our five children. Hudson and Dawn, you trudged through the hardest chapters of this book with me. Your young hopeful lives gave me a reason to survive and the courage to continue pressing on. Hudson, I am proud of the strong adult you have become as you are impacting the world around you in a brilliant way, and Dawn, you have that same passion to inspire, making a difference within your sphere of influence. Tanner, you have been dealt a hard hand in life, and yet by God's grace, you have overcome and proven that yes, ALL things can work together for the good.

My Michael, every day I am grateful to the Lord for sending me an innately good and God-fearing man who loves me unconditionally and has faithfully walked beside me down this long road towards health and wholeness. Thank you for providing us with stability and giving me the joy of being a mom again with the birth of our sons, Joffrey and Stefan.

To my son, Joffrey, who is now with our Lord in heaven—you have set the standard for true courage as a young adult bravely facing your terminal cancer diagnosis. I will always miss your infectious laughter and joyful spirit—looking forward to the day we meet again in the next life.

Stefan, you are the youngest but have always been wise beyond your years. Thank you for your support through my hard years of grief, so I could get to the point of writing this story—always lightening it up by entertaining me with your incredible intellect and hysterical wit. You truly are a guiding "STAR."

AND ... my life and this book would not exist without my little friend, **Re-**.

I give glory to God for "her," HIS Amazing **GRACE**.

I praise my Lord Jesus Christ for His gift of forgiveness for all my sins: past, present, & future.

Foreword

WHEN I REFLECT on how much has happened since I first met Rebecca in 2009, I am taken aback by God's faithfulness. Let me share a bit about how we first met. In 2007, I began teaching group exercise classes, then received personal training, yoga, and Pilates equipment certifications. Rebecca graciously hired me at her large studio, Get Reformed Pilates, in Frisco, Texas. At the time, my husband, Coleman, served as a youth minister and was pursuing a master's degree in theology at Dallas Theological Seminary (DTS). I served in the youth ministry alongside him while I also trained clients and taught classes full time.

As I continued to serve both the youth and their families in ministry and help my fitness clients with their goals, the Lord grew my desire to care for others from a holistic perspective. This led me to pursue a masters in biblical counseling at DTS as well. Later, my husband and I both received our doctorates from The Southern Baptist Theological Seminary.

Rebecca and I share an incredible desire to help and support others on their path towards health and wellness. Rebecca's own passion to help others become the best versions of themselves has been made evident throughout her life, within the dance and fitness realm, as well as in her many other circles of influence. If you ask her though, she will tell you that she credits the Spirit of God for gradually changing her from someone who was critical and self-centered to someone who is more others-centered. As someone who has been the recipient of her continual care and encouragement, I can tell you that she has played a pivotal role in my life, and I know this is the case for many others, as you will see as she tells her story.

The Lord has worked in and through her in tremendous ways over the years that I have known her. In 2010, at age 19, her son Joffrey was diagnosed with a rare terminal sarcoma cancer. This devastating news was a shock to the entire Get Reformed Pilates family. Yet, Rebecca's faith remained strong through the trials that came as a result of his diagnosis. Coleman and I were fortunate to have the opportunity to befriend Joffrey, as well as his girlfriend, Christina. Joffrey and Christina made the decision to be married "in the Lord" despite his terminal diagnosis. Coleman had the privilege of officiating at their wedding, and what a glorious celebration it was! I still remember the beauty of the outdoor ceremony and how the happy couple beamed with excitement, exchanged rings, and vowed "till death do us part."

Foreword

The heartbreak of Joffrey's passing six months later at age 22 left a long and lasting impact on the entire community. Coleman officiated the funeral, which was a privilege and an honor. As we walked alongside Rebecca and her family through that season, I wondered how could a mother process their son being diagnosed with a terminal cancer, then grieve the loss of her beloved child and still press on? Now that I am a mother of two, I cannot even imagine all that she endured. As you will see through Rebecca's story, it is her strong faith that has sustained her. She trusted in God's goodness because she had experienced it time and time again throughout her life.

From tragedy to triumph and all that has been in between, God's grace upheld Rebecca, and her little 2-letter friend, **Re-,** was always beside her. I am beyond grateful that you are holding this book because in reading it, you will experience God's great faithfulness through Rebecca's story. I know that her determination and perseverance rooted in the Lord will be an encouragement to you as you read. Be assured that the events in our lives are not independent of each other. Just as we are whole and integrated people created by God and in His image, our lives should also be seen from a holistic point of view. Know that God will use each and every single thing that you and I have endured to make us into who we are today. None of our suffering or trials are wasted. God will redeem them! In this beautifully crafted memoir, you will be reminded that the Lord uses all things for our good and for His glory (Romans 8:28). As you read, remember that our experiences shape us—the challenging, the good, and the normal everyday moments. They have a purpose, and again, they play a part in making us who we are at this very moment. Be inspired by Rebecca's courageous story, then, be sure to pass it along to others who need this same encouragement in their lives.

"The steadfast love of the Lord never ceases; His mercies never come to an end; they are new every morning; great is Your faithfulness" (Lamentations 3:22-23).

With joy,
Alexandria Ford, Ed.D.
Certified Health and Wellness Coach, Cultivate Well

Introduction

Yes! ***You ARE going to get through THIS because…***

*"The will of God will not take us
where the grace of God cannot sustain us."[1]*
(Evangelist Billy Graham)

Who is **Re-**?
She is my personification of God's **Grace**.
Dr. *Tony Evans simply defines* **Grace** *as "the inexhaustible
supply of God's goodness whereby He does for us what
we could never do for ourselves. It is His gift to us."[2]*

Looking back, I see that my little friend **Re-** has been weaving her threads of lovingkindness throughout my life, wooing me closer and closer to that ledge of faith until I finally fell off, caught by her lifesaving net.

Grace knew me long before I found her. She is familiar with the years of my agonizing struggle to find self-worth in an environment of critical and conditional love. Unknown to me, she was there at each low point, gently prodding me to keep seeking the reason to keep going on in life, even when I continued to fail myself and others.

Re- was there at my first birth, my second birth, and all the days of light and darkness in between.

Introduction

*Years before time, God had set His mind
on one small grain of sand out of the billions He had planned.
He determined by His will how He would
slowly fashion this grain of sand.
When time finally was born, this small
grain came into being ... but before
it could even acknowledge its surroundings ...
it was locked up in darkness.
Why in darkness Lord? Why separated from the light of Your
presence? Why?
There was a struggle ... there was seeking
and a reaching out ... then ...
God said, 'NOW!' and the oyster was opened by HIS gentle
hand ...
the light of day revealed no grain of sand ...
rather a pearl.
The Lord took her in His hands ...
You are one of my priceless treasures,* **REBECCA**
*I have loved you from the beginning,
and
I will love you to
the end.*

(Author Unknown)

Chapter 1

THE CALL

December 1986

I COULD NOT BELIEVE THAT the local TV station would send their crew on a Saturday morning to the Rapides Parish Library to film clips of my student mini production of "Nutcracker in a Nutshell," but then I guess this was a newsworthy event for small town, small time Alexandria ... Alexandria, LOUISIANA that is! Moving here from the Chicago area five years before was like jumping backwards through a time warp 20 years; back to the mindset of the mid 1960s.

There was a set of railroad tracks dividing the town, literally and figuratively.

I am sure that my best friend from Chicago, a professional woman of color, would not have felt equally welcome here. Even in 1986, racial lines were not crossed, policing and politics predictably followed the *good 'ole boy code*, most well-bred women still knew their proper place in society, and gossip was rampant. The local newspaper was aptly named the *Town Talk*. The crime rate was high; the school rankings were low; the air quality was lousy, and a taste for the finer arts—classical ballet, music, and theatre—was still being acquired. Thus, I endeavored to be somewhat of a missionary for the arts, bringing ballet to the people. With all these given negatives about the town, I bet you're asking, "Why stay?" The fishing and the hunting can't be that good! But what if I told you that the people there are extraordinary, that yes, they are THAT good? Well … most of them anyway.

My two small children, Hudson and Dawn, couldn't have been any more excited, sitting in front of our tiny TV as we waited to see ourselves on the five o'clock newsfeed. Seated behind the kids on my grandmother's hand-me-down loveseat, I couldn't help but take that moment to reflect on the scene of the Christmas miracle in front of me: well, first there was ME—still alive, then my treasured carved baby Jesus asleep in his wooden manger on top of the coffee table, and yes, there were my precious children with me, giggling and shivering together on the cold hardwood floor in our living room all wrapped up in their favorite blankies. I was back in my home again. Who would believe so much could change since that

The Call

November day over a year ago when I sat on Jan Pierce's couch in Conroe, Texas, totally hopeless, and my hand desperately clutching a loaded gun?

NOW!

"NOW!" is a powerful word. It is the exact, precise present moment. There is everything before now and there is all that comes after. Some "nows" are tragic and irreversible, such as the depressed moment my older brother, Larry, squeezed the trigger on the gun pointed to his head and ended his life at age 34, leaving behind a lovely wife and their precious six-month-old daughter. My own daughter was born just three weeks after the funeral, and our family has carried the guilt and sadness of that suicide for all these years after that decisive "now" and wished we could have somehow changed that choice to a "never!"

Some "nows" can be witnessed and recorded and celebrated ... Olympic records broken by a thousandth of a second, times of birth/death written on certificates, a mental "wow" moment where ideas are crystalized and life purposes are revealed. Most "nows" are quiet and mysterious acts of God ... when was the exact time of your physical conception when a specific sperm and egg united to uniquely create you? When did you notice that your spirit was now alive to God, not a physical birth, but a spiritual birth, "**re**born"?

My "now" moment was neither quiet nor secret. It was ridiculously dramatic, unlikely, and unexpected.

Ever read in the Bible about the Apostle Paul's radical experience on the famous "Road to Damascus"? He was slammed to the ground and blindsided by a post-resurrection appearance of the Lord Jesus. That encounter turned his life 180 degrees in the opposite direction from persecuting Christians to becoming a Christ follower. This same Paul is the author of at least 13 books in the New Testament. Yes ... wow!

OK, so I wouldn't really compare myself to St. Paul, but what happened on that "couch in Conroe" was likewise a radical conversion! My dancer friend, Jan Pierce, who met me a decade before, back in 1975 when I moved from Dallas to Conroe, knew me then by my childhood nickname, *"Becky."* Jan witnessed such an instantaneous inner change in me right after that miraculous "born again" experience that she began calling me "**Re**-Becky," or the "**NEW** 2.0 version of Becky," as her special way of recognizing the immediate results of God's effectual call on my life in that moment in time. *Now*, back to the future and the TV newscast.

The Interruption

"Mommy, Mommy! That's you talking in your red shirt." Dawn jumped up to run and point to the TV-me as I was explaining to the mostly young audience how ballet dancers must practice every day at the ballet barre ... a quick clip of my students performing a choreographed demo of barre work set to a Chopin piece. Then, more TV-me talk and visuals of three dancers in long white bell shaped romantic "tutus" dancing a version of "Carol of the Bells." Hudson joined Dawn in the jubilant bouncing as the familiar "Nutcracker" music came through the TV speakers. The camera zoomed in to show me turning the pages in a giant coloring book, as I narrated the magical story of Clara and the Nutcracker Prince.

"Mommy, look me, see me," Dawn gleefully shouted, as she pointed to her 3 ½-year-old Littlest Angel self on the screen playing the harp and leading the Sugar Plum Fairy to the Kingdom of Sweets where the Arabians, Chinese, Reed Flutes, and Russians all dance for her. Yes! There was Hudson as a tumbling Russian. He had made it perfectly through his leaping somersault routine, but during his final bows he had walked backwards smack into the tower of stacked library chairs, falling onto the floor. Oh, thank goodness—they edited out that tumble, saving his five-year-old pride!

I had pride too … as their teacher. I was pleased to see my students embrace the more rigorous training and standards of classical ballet and perform so well given our relatively short window of rehearsal time. However, I could not take any credit for the training of my Sugar Plum ballerina, Sue, who looked exquisite in my hot pink tutu. She was a talented dancer who just dropped out of the sky and landed nearby at England Air Force base, where her husband was recently stationed. He was supportive of her ballet aspirations and came to the performance along with one of his handsome Air Force buddies.

I twinged a bit when I saw that the TV camera picked up a profile shot of his friend standing next to me in the aftermath of the afternoon performance as the crowd chatted with the performers, expressing their appreciation for our show. Later, as we were gathering our costumes and bags, Sue came up to me and said that her husband's friend was infatuated with me. He wanted to know if I would join them for dinner. I was stunned. I had never thought about another relationship … I wasn't even legally divorced yet. I was still a "married" woman, and I held onto the slim hope that my husband and I would **re**concile. I told her to tell him, "Thank you, but NO. I couldn't do that right now." I never actually spoke to him myself or heard his voice. I wasn't sure if I felt flattered or a little freaked that he was "infatuated" with me … not a safe word choice.

The kids were still skipping around the room reliving their moment of dance fame when the phone in the kitchen rang, as the evening news was concluding. It was probably one of the other thrilled moms who saw her own child dancing on TV and thought to call me to share in our mutual excitement. I ran into the kitchen to grab the receiver off the wall before I missed **THE CALL**.

"Hello," I breathlessly answered, expecting to hear a woman's voice.

"Hi Becky! I just saw you on TV," I heard a man's voice say to me.

I didn't recognize the voice, and most of all—no one here in Alexandria knows me by my nickname, "Becky"! Only my family, childhood friends in Dallas, and folks from my pre-Chicago days (before 1979) will still call me "Becky," and I can tell by the clear, static-free tone that this is not a long-distance call.

"You looked great in your red shirt and ballet tights, moving around explaining ballet to everyone," he continued while I still struggled to match the voice with a memory.

"I missed it; who did you say this is?" I said.

He ignored my question and went on with his side of the conversation, "I liked seeing you on TV. You looked nice up in front of everybody, like you were having a good time."

"Excuse me—who is this? Do we know each other?" I asked him again, "I'm sorry, but I don't think I recognize your voice."

"I bet you're a beautiful ballerina too—I hope next time I'll see you dance with your students," he further informed me. Without pausing he continued, "Yes, I enjoyed watching you … you look like you would be a lot of fun to **"F - - -,"** he arrogantly announced to me.

"Ohhhhh DISGUSTING!!!" I shouted as I slammed the receiver back down.

*Men are such **JERKS**, I thought to myself. What's your problem? Don't you have anything better to do than make obscene phone calls? You make me sick! Get a life! I'm working four jobs trying to take care of my kids to make a living. You invade my private home with your STUPID phone call—trying to ruin what should be a happy celebration with my children? You **JERK**!!*

That's what I wish I had said to him before I hung up.

"Mommy," both the kids exclaimed as they heard me

shouting and came running into the kitchen. "Who was on the phone?"

"Nobody," I assured them. "Just a STUPID person".

"Ahh," they nodded, but in their little preschool minds they wondered. Mommy never allowed them to name-call each other or anybody else, STUPID.

That was the first **CALL** that I can remember, one where he spoke to me.

Where I heard that **VOICE** for the first time.

Chapter 2

THE DALLAS COWBOYS CONNECTION

When Becky met Joyce

1976 WAS A SIGNIFICANT YEAR for some of us. Tom Landry, the iconic coach for the Dallas Cowboys, hired Dr. Bob Ward as the first fulltime Strength and Conditioning coach in the NFL. Who could have known then, that at age 45, Dr. Ward would be the one "changing the trajectory of sports and the people in them"?[3] He introduced his innovative program: individualized computer-generated workouts for each player, emphasizing diet and flexibility as well as running and weightlifting. Randy White, Cowboys Defensive tackle, 1975-88 and Pro Football Hall of Famer said, "... we see Bob Ward everywhere. The man impacted the NFL Combine, the NFL Draft, player analysis and evaluation, workouts, even how a football player takes water breaks."[4]

Dr. Bob Ward is known as "the man who brought science to football," according to Dr. James Disch, Professor of Biomechanics at Rice University.[5] Bob created new equipment and methods to be able to transfer the strength and power developed in training to the playing field. He was an innovator in that he introduced his players to martial arts, yoga, ballet—any movement discipline that would give them an edge. Butch Johnson, wide receiver with the Cowboys and the Broncos said of Bob, "What he brought to the NFL was a combination of track, weightlifting, and power lifting. The CrossFit craze you see today? That is Bob Ward's workout ... This is not new. It's 40 years old."[6] Dr. Ward moved to Dallas from California with his wife, Joyce, and teenage daughter, leaving the older daughter there to pursue her upper education. This is where my life path providentially intersected with the brilliantly gifted and gracious Ward family—changing me, positively impacting my personal life and career to this very day.

Ah YES! And **1976** was also the year "The Wink" was born and forever changed the nation's view of sports. Superbowl X was in Miami between the Pittsburgh Steelers and the Cowboys. CBS was televising the game and made a concerted effort to feature the Dallas Cowboy Cheerleaders in what would become known as "Honey Shots"—close ups of the cheerleaders in their revealing uniforms. When one of those Cowboy Cheerleaders winked at the camera, the nation forgot there was a football game going on, and the potential for "sports as entertainment" was acknowledged. The Dallas Cowboy Cheerleaders became the symbol of female empowerment and sexual freedom—the second wave of women's evolving identity.[7]

1976 was also the year my mother, Beth, died. December 23. We buried her on Christmas Eve. She was only 47 years old. I was just 23. It was scleroderma, an autoimmune disease which gradually hardens the connective tissues in the body—she had been battling it for 20 years. Muscle is connective tissue; the heart is a muscle; her heart couldn't contract to pump anymore. My mother had the biggest heart for people: she was gorgeous, talented, determined, and full of life and creative energy. That October, I drove up to Dallas from Conroe for her birthday. She was in the hospital for a complication from hip surgery. I gave her the framed needlepoint piece I had been working on during road trips and rehearsals. It summed up her approach to life. In large, loud, orange letters surrounded by flowers it read, *"Creative Mess is Better Than Stagnant Neatness"*.

I also brought the hot pink tutu she had sewn for a ballet recital of mine years ago. She sat up in bed to draw out the design and then laid out the beaded jewels for me to pin and later sew onto the velvet bodice. She transformed it into my *Sugar Plum Fairy* costume for the first "Nutcracker in a Nutshell" performances I would be directing and dancing in throughout the schools with the *Woodlands Ballet Company*, a small civic ballet troupe my friend Jan Pierce and I founded.

Lots of little girls in Dallas at the time I grew up had the raw talent to become professional ballet dancers, but they didn't all have a mother like mine who sacrificed to drive me miles across town every day to the Dallas Civic Ballet studio and wait there for four to five hours for me to finish classes and rehearsals. She was one of the first "working mothers" among my friends, and she eventually had her own showroom at the Dallas Apparel Mart carrying lines of children's clothes. She paid for my expensive pointe shoes.

She never pushed me. We shared our love for the performing arts. We bonded through those experiences together. She supported me when I graduated from high school and immediately left for Cannes, France, to train as an apprentice to the *L'Opera de Ballet* company in Marseilles. She was understanding when I was injured overseas, returned to the States, then decided to stay and pursue my BFA in dance from Southern Methodist University. Mother was naturally proud when, a year after graduation, I joined the *Dallas Ballet Ensemble* for their inaugural season as a fully professional company with my dance mentor, Artistic Director George Skibine.

Dance, Sports, & God

Where am I going with all this??! Oh yeah ... how did I get connected to the Cowboys' coach and his family? The answer is dance! It is the inexplicable passion for dance that binds together those of us blessed and cursed with the compulsion to move-express-create. And the answer also is sports and athletics! Dr. Ward was trained as an athlete/educator, but his wife, Joyce, was a dancer/educator—a woman after my own heart.

Our lives crossed at Main & Elm Street in downtown Dallas (a few steps from the infamous "Triple Underpass" where JFK was shot) in the Dance Department of El Centro Community College. Joyce had just joined the faculty there and at Booker T. Washington, Dallas's renowned Performing Arts High School. I was serving the City of Dallas as their first Dance Artist-in-Residence, and since I had to report to City Hall downtown, El Centro was an ideal location for me to take ballet and modern dance classes to stay in performing condition.

I Found My Mother's Heart In Joyce

Joyce Ward and I instantly connected because of our mutual passions: for dance, athletics, people, and the God who created them! I found my mother's heart in her. Joyce understood the conflict I felt between my devotion to the art of dance and my devotion to God and the tensions they created in my life and marriage. Joyce for sure could hold her own with Big D's beautiful people crowd of the time. She was extremely attractive with a fit dancer's body, but what drew me to her was not only her joyful countenance and full-out enthusiasm for the latest project at hand, but her authenticity as a Christian woman.

Her personal strengths were a package deal—ALL the fruit of the Spirit: *"love, joy, peace, patience, kindness, goodness, faithfulness, gentleness, self-control"* (Galatians 5:22). Well truthfully, she might have been lacking occasionally in the self-control category ... we were known to stay up all night furiously driven to finish a dance or fitness project and snacking our way through it ... if you were lucky enough to find any real food in the Wards' cabinets, not just protein powder and vitamins! On the other hand, her husband, Bob, was the admirable epitome of self-discipline in his personal fitness and nutritional program.

The quality in Joyce that has always stood out the most to me is her non-judgmental approach to people, her unconditional and accepting love for them ... for me. At first, I thought it was just a Southern California thing. She didn't try to "fix" me or criticize me, even when I was in the middle of my ugliest struggles. She extended herself to me in compassionate understanding, looking past my flawed self to see my giftedness and who I could become ... the woman God uniquely created me to be.

*Joyce was the first person who revealed **"Re-"** to me. She is a Christian woman who is full of **Grace**.* She has always been loving and non-condemning, even when I wasn't following the perfect list of good and godly behavior. She showed me how to forgive myself and move on in God's forgiveness until I could find that **grace** for myself ... she kept me moving forward on my long journey towards the Lord and that ledge.

Joyce encouraged me not to keep burying myself under my self-made funeral pyre of failures. Perfectionism is perhaps the universal curse of all classical ballerinas, and I still struggle to be free from those chains:

> *Not that I have already obtained it or have already become perfect, but **I press on** so that I may lay hold of that for which also I was laid hold of by Christ Jesus ... I do not regard myself as having laid hold of it yet; but one thing I do: **forgetting what lies behind** and reaching forward to what lies ahead, **I PRESS ON** toward the goal for the prize of the upward call of God in Christ Jesus (Philippians 3:12-14, emphasis mine).*

When I first met her husband, Bob, I was impressed of course with his status as a Dallas Cowboys coach, and he lived up to my expectations with his athletic appearance—superman handsome and well-built, but I was pleasantly surprised by his quiet and humble spirit ... what a combination! He was not at all the stereotype of the egotistical "jock" that I was expecting. Oh, did I mention that he is CRAZY SMART??—literally, a genius ahead of his time. Joyce and I both laughed at how we could never keep up with his conversations as he attempted to explain the physics of "speed and explosion" or expound upon his latest top shelf training theories. We are dancer right-brain dominant creatures, but Dr. Ward's brain operates full power on all cylinders. Bob was a part of the Christian culture that existed within the Cowboy organization during the Coach Tom Landry era…coaches, players, and wives voluntarily attended Bible studies and prayed together.

> The Wards have been lifelong role models for me showing me how to compete in this world and strive for uncompromising excellence, **without abandoning your Christian values and lifestyle.**

Chapter 3

IT'S FUN TO STAY AT THE YWCA!

Meet My Steel Magnolias

HOME ANSWERING MACHINES were available after AT&T broke up in 1984, and they became a regular household necessity for those who could afford them, which was NOT me. I was still piecing together an income with the guidance from two key strong and influential women in my life, the YWCA's program director, Ann Masden, and the executive director, Denise Van Bibber. I had met Denise back in the spring of '86 at Alexandria Day School where she was the P.E. teacher, and I was newly separated from my husband and looking for work. I had spent the spring as a permanent substitute English teacher at a high school, but without the proper certifications, I couldn't count on continual employment teaching English, so I had to fall back on my area of expertise, the dance/fitness sector.

Denise was technically middle age, but she still maintained her striking good looks—tall, lean, and athletic with stylish, short dark hair. She had an outgoing, and some would say a rather dominating, personality that made you want to say, "Yes sir, Coach!" when she asked me to do something. She had a generous, helpful spirit and gave me a gig teaching dance movement to the gymnastic team at the day school. I also privately coached her sweet teenage daughter for some beauty and talent competitions, which, by the way, she nailed! Denise was going through a transition from teaching. She was getting over the shock of what was a national tragedy when on January 28, 1986, the space shuttle, *Challenger*, blew up 73 seconds off the launch pad, killing the five astronauts and two payload specialists, one of whom was Christa McAuliffe, part of NASA's first "Teacher in Space" program.[8] Denise had earned a position as a finalist for that teacher program, so the disaster was especially personal for her.

When word got out that the YWCA was looking for a new director with energy and a vision, Denise thought it would be a good fit—a change from teaching but still giving her opportunities to impact young lives. First thing she did was hire a very capable director of programming, her friend, Ann Masden, who had just gone through her own personal tragedy, losing her teenage daughter to cancer. In contrast to Denise, Ann was shorter in stature, but then, next to Denise, we were all short!

She had soft, short brown hair and bluish-gray eyes that could either highlight that soft blue hue or turn that steely gray when staring you down! Ms. Masden always dressed professionally … maybe *business casual* as we would say now. Discreet, small jewelry pieces—nothing big and colorfully loud—always in fine taste. *Organized, skilled communicator, insightful, long-range vision, and persistent* are words I would put on her business profile, but as a person, she was still a mom in a pantsuit … considerate, caring, and approachable.

When I say these women were STRONG, I mean God could not have placed any better "*Steel Magnolias,*"[9] in my life … strong, yet vulnerable. Even in ways I could not see at the time, God was quietly leading me, weaving people and circumstances into my new **Re**-Becky life to bring about the **GOOD** He had planned for me:

"*And we know that God causes all things to work together for good to those who love God, to those who are called according to His purpose*" (Romans 8:28).

My Life Coach

As program director, it was Ms. Masden who became my boss when I began teaching ballet, aerobic, and gymnastic classes at the YW in the summer of 1986. I was rather spoiled and artistically independent, so maybe I had never worked under someone who really kept on top of me. Ms. Ann gave me a well needed dose of tough love.

Her answering machine in the office worked just fine, and if there were calls from parents who had problems with how I handled their children in classes, I was brought in right away, and the issue was discussed. "So how in the future could I better deal with the child?" she would propose to me ... but that would be AFTER I returned the call to the parent, apologized, and accepted responsibility. I painfully remember one incident which involved a woman in one of my aerobic classes. Evidently, in trying to be humorous while teaching, I said something that really offended the woman and hurt her feelings. When Ms. Ann told me what this woman was feeling because of what I said, I just broke down and cried ... how could I be so arrogant and insensitive that I would discourage a woman when my heart was only to help her? Ms. Ann gently broke the news about me to me—sometimes when I'm trying to be confident in front of people, I can come off as cocky and full of myself. *Ouch!*

We didn't use the term back then, but if we did, I would have called Ms. Masden my "Life Coach." Did I mention she was tough? She was, but it was because she saw my possibilities and wanted to develop me into that better, stronger woman I could become.

She was extraordinarily kind to my two little ones and made all sorts of accommodations for me to be able to work and not have to pay for childcare. The kids were enrolled in the programming on scholarship. Dawn would sit on a mat and play with her toys in the mornings while I taught, and Ms.

Ann let them wait for me at the back of the room sometimes during the 15-minute gap between the end of the after-school program and the end of my classes. Ann was a person of the highest integrity whose genuine Catholic Christian faith was evident in the smallest details of her life … she taught me that the Lord desires and requires utter honesty. I was struggling to provide for the kids … child support at that time in Louisiana was $125 per month per child for everything—food, housing, clothes, school, etc., and they were often hungry while waiting for me to finish teaching. The cabinet with the after-school program snacks did not have a lock, and sometimes I would grab some peanut butter crackers or other snacks for them. The YWCA was doing so much to help us that I didn't really think of it as stealing, but as Ms. Ann pointed out to me later, it was. They were glad to help in whatever way possible, but she also had a budget she was accountable for and supplies to order for the after-school program. When I took snacks without asking, that affected her and the program. *Ouch!*

Just another "Lesson from Ms. Ann"—it is **NOT** all about me!

Chapter 4

F.U.N. FITNESS SYSTEMS

Birth of a Business

IT WAS MS. MASDEN who came up with the idea that I should start a fitness business ... of course it was her! The opportunity was there for me to conduct weekend fitness certification seminars for instructors. I had been traveling back and forth from Alexandria to Dallas since the spring of 1983, right after Dawn was born, to work with Joyce Ward. Joyce had invited me to come learn the aerobic group exercise program she had created combining HER talent as a dancer/choreographer and BOB'S knowledge of exercise science. She knew I was breaking away from my ballerina image because of my anorexia and looking for the more normal and healthy body image I saw in the exercise world. I had begun teaching my first classes in the fellowship hall of my church, then expanded to the local health club. I had trained a select few to assist me as teachers of Joyce's program, but was I ready to go big with it?

The 1980'S Aerobics Craze
Joyce & Me

It was NUTS! Dallas was mania central. The Dallas Cowboy Cheerleaders were a phenomenon, and Joyce hired the former head cheerleader, Debbie C. as her lead teacher-trainer. It was the wild, wild west where anything goes—no heart rate monitoring, no safe exercise protocols … it was **FUN** … and dangerous. In the beginning, there was no such thing as a "certification;" anyone could teach aerobic exercise! Starting my own exercise certification business in Louisiana was smart. Thanks, Ann!

While I was in Dallas visiting family for Christmas in 1986, right after that "Nutcracker in a Nutshell" at the Alexandria library with the children, I got away to go visit Bob and Joyce. We laid the foundation for a business collaboration I named **F.U.N. Fitness Systems** (**F**itness **U**nited with **N**utrition). This became another major income piece in my ongoing challenge of being a working single mom with a goal of not putting my children in traditional day care but bringing them with me to work, and now, working on the weekends when they were with my ex for visitation.

 Ms. Masden set up my first certification weekend at the YWCA in Natchitoches, Louisiana—the historical European style settlement, the oldest city from the Louisiana Purchase, and by the way, this city was the location where the movie "Steel Magnolias" was filmed. She put me up in a gorgeous two-story bed & breakfast with a claw foot bathtub in my room and a Sunday morning brunch in the parlor, accompanied by a jazz musician playing on the baby grand piano. The accommodations were a dream, but my seminar was a real disaster.

 I cringe when I remember what an awful job I did and how unprepared I was. I stayed up through the night before I left Alexandria putting together training manuals, but when I got there to hand them out and begin, the pages were all in the wrong order, and that was only the beginning of the confusion. I had no experience in conducting fitness tests in a large group: calculating resting heart rates or the target heart zone or administering the 12-minute run, timed push-ups, and sit-ups. I was still transforming myself from "Genteel Ballerina" to "Bad Ass Fitness Coach." I didn't understand how to manage my time to be able to squeeze all the material in over the weekend, so a huge chunk was left out, and there was no time to give the complete final "Test-Out" to the participants, but I signed and handed out their F.U.N. Fitness System Certificates anyway.

 It was a sham, and I was ashamed to come back to Ms. Masden and tell her what a failure I was, especially after all she did to help me get started. As you could guess from what I've already told you about her . . .

- She didn't shame me, but neither did she give me any sympathy.
- She rebuked me for being stubborn and not asking for help to get the materials ready for the seminar.
- She more gently reproved me for not practicing my presentation and laying out a schedule.

> "... preach the word; be ready in season and out of season; reprove, rebuke, exhort, with great patience and instruction" (II Timothy 4:2).

What I got from her was the "locker room after a loss" speech: a confidence-building exhortation to get back to work and fix the problems—all rolled into one talk and then, a quick boot out her office door. Done! That was classic Ms. Ann.

I knew I had to learn how to take the strict discipline I had acquired during my training as a classical ballerina and transfer it to the world of sports/business—it was hard and knocked me all out of joint:

> "All discipline for the moment seems not to be joyful, but sorrowful; yet to those who have been trained by it, afterwards it yields the peaceful fruit of righteousness. Therefore, strengthen the hands that are weak and the knees that are feeble, and make straight paths for your

feet, so the limb which is lame may not be put out of joint, but rather be healed" (Hebrews 12:11-12).

Somehow by God's **GRACE** my business survived. Participation in my F.U.N. Certifications grew in numbers until I had to rent the gym at the LSU-Alexandria campus to accommodate everyone. The university there had an opening for an "adjunct teacher in dance & aerobic exercise," and although I only had a BFA in dance, I thought I had a chance of landing the position because I had already taught P.E./dance at El Centro Community College in Dallas. They asked for a letter of recommendation, so I phoned Dr. Ward and asked if he minded mailing me a letter which I could give to the school along with my application.

The Gift Of Encouragement

When his letter arrived in the middle of June 1987, I experienced the transcendent power that his positive words of affirmation brought to my hurting soul, which was filled with self-doubts ... starved for reasons to believe that I had value, that I had worth, and that it is worthwhile to continue the struggle. I had to find the guts to follow the vision and keep seeking the purpose for which God had specifically created me. Dr. Bob Ward's letter was written on fine stationary with the impressive Dallas Cowboys logo, the famous blue star, and address across the top.

Re- *and* Me

TO WHOM IT MAY CONCERN:

I can highly recommend Rebecca XXXX for the position of adjunct teacher at LSU-A in dance and aerobic exercise.

Her training, experience, and abilities in dance are well recognized in Dallas, and she has worked extensively with the aerobic exercise program developed by Bob Ward Enterprises.

Rebecca's energy and enthusiasm and zeal for learning, her attention to detail, her knowledge of the body and how it moves gained from her years of dance training, her teaching and organizational experience, and her own personal commitment to physical fitness all assure her success in being able to provide outstanding classes in your Physical Education Department.

I certainly have confidence in her skills and teaching ability to fulfill your position.

Sincerely,

DALLAS COWBOYS FOOTBALL CLUB
Bob Ward, P.E.D.
Conditioning Coach

From the day that letter arrived in 1987 until today, I have been inspired and humbled to try and be "my utmost for His highest; my best for His glory" as Oswald Chambers describes our God-given purpose.[10] Dr. Ward's letter boosted my confidence because his sincere words expressed belief in me and my abilities. Even though I didn't believe that about myself, I knew that Dr. Ward was trustworthy, a man of integrity who did not flatter but only spoke truth. He was able to do a good thing for me by thoughtfully crafting those words and taking the time and effort to put them on paper and mail them. His words encouraged me. His efforts to help me succeed quietly exhorted me to press on. I didn't get that job, but I kept his letter.

Dr. Ward taught me much by his example, and today, in my smaller ways, I try to speak, email, text, and send cards that communicate support and send words of encouragement into the souls of those who receive them. I know from this experience that well-chosen words, simple words from a sincere heart, can lift a person up.

"But encourage one another day after day, as long as it is still called 'Today'..." (Hebrews 3:13).

Chapter 5

THE VOICE

August 1987

My Confession

ONE HOT, HUMID Friday afternoon in mid-August, I brought my children to the YWCA where my best friend from church, Phyllis Word, would meet me. Ms. Masden allowed them to join "free play" with the summer campers, so I could quietly slip out of their sight without tears and separation drama. Phyllis arrived, and we transferred Hudson and Dawn's car seats, their suitcases, toys, and special "blankies" to her station wagon. She assured me they would be well cared for at her place. I hated to miss my weekend with the children, but it was unavoidable. Joyce Ward was flying in from Dallas as my "celebrity guest" to lead the F.U.N. Fitness Certification weekend, and this was the only date she had available. After the children were safely on the road with Phyllis to Pineville, I had a few spare moments—just long enough for a quick conversation with Ms. Ann.

I knocked and asked if we could talk privately. I closed her door, and without taking a breath, I blurted out what I had been holding in for the past nine months, "I have been receiving obscene phone calls with relentless regularity since that first phone call during the *Nutcracker* newscast last December. When I was renting that duplex near the Owl Grocery, before I moved back into my home, I also remember answering the phone and hearing only heavy breathing, but no voice. After the *Nutcracker* call to my home, when mystery guy first spoke, this JERK has continued to call me ... maybe a few times a month. You know how crazy and chaotic my life is. I've had no time to dwell on it; it's been a blip on my radar. But now ... it's different. After my ad ran in the *Town Talk* for the fitness seminar, the closer it gets to this weekend, the shorter the time between his calls!"

Believing that she thought I was being a bit melodramatic, I then walked it back some and apologetically added, "I find it mostly annoying ... no big deal. I just put his calls in the same category as the prank phone call we would make when we were in middle school but without the bad language!"

"No," Ms. Ann said, "I don't think these calls fit in the same category as a prank call. Tell me a bit more. Do you have time?"

The Voice

"Well," I confided in her, "it's always the same voice, the same breathing. He talks to me in a familiar way, as if we had a relationship, then sometimes he starts to say inappropriate things to me, and I quickly hang up before I can hear what he says. I quit trying to engage him altogether or listen when I hear it is his voice right after I pick up the phone. I tell him, 'STOP calling me!' and then I hang up and move on."

"But now," I told Ms. Ann, "my heart skips that beat every time the phone rings. I know I must answer it … it could be a call about the kids or important news from Dallas about my family. When I hear his voice, I get mad. I'm irritated. Frustrated. You know how busy I am. I'm just thinking about feeding the kids, getting them bathed, and putting them to bed. Then I have work to do. I have no time for this guy's stupid game! What should I do? What can the police do about the phone calls? Will they think I'm some silly female who can't hang up a phone?"

I thought I recognized a shade of alarm behind her usually calm, controlled exterior, but Ms. Ann held my hand and reassured me, "Yes, you should call the police and tell them all this. They will take it seriously." *Hmmm … she knows something I don't know … she reads the newspapers … she watches the daily TV news.* I promised her that as soon as I got through the weekend fitness certification seminar, I would make a report to the police, so they could do something about JERKY guy.

Re- *and* Me

The Single Mom Life

DONE! It was late Saturday afternoon and we were finished. The fitness certification seminar was a success. Joyce was incredible. Everyone loved her and her F.U.N. aerobic program. Her presence gave me the credibility I needed to move my business forward to a larger audience. I was unbelievably grateful once more for God's **GRACE**—for putting Joyce and the Ward family in my life. Emotionally, I was on a high, feeling the favor of the Lord and the fruits of our hard work. The *Town Talk* newspaper sent a staff reporter to interview us after the event and take photos for the Sunday morning news. I said my good-byes to Joyce, who had to catch her plane back to Dallas, then I loaded up all the materials from the seminar and drove home alone. The front porch light was still out, so it was easier to roll on down the long driveway along the side of the house and pull up to the back door. I was beat. I transferred all the stuff from the car into the small ballet studio at the back of the house and went to my bedroom to change out of my aerobic clothes.

My bedroom was a mess. It doubled as my office, and I had a long folding table against the window that served as my desk, stacked with training notebooks and a pile of cassette tapes next to my electric typewriter. I couldn't afford curtains, so there were sheets nailed up to my window frame and thumb tacks holding it into the side wall, but often there were gaps in my homemade curtain when the tacks gave way. I would work at my office "desk" late into the night after putting the children to bed, and occasionally, I would imagine noises outside my window, but I pushed any fearful thoughts aside to focus on my work.

The hour now was late—too late to go pick up the children in Pineville. They would already be in bed. Instead, I called them, gave them their "nite-nite talk" and promised I would meet them in the morning at church with their donuts! Phyllis was the dearest person I had ever met; always there to help, to serve, to listen. She had so many of the wonderful qualities that I admired but lacked … patience, kindness, generosity, and unselfishness, to name a few. Sunday morning, she dressed my two kids, packed all their stuff into their car and along with her husband and their three kids, met me at church. Many of us talk about sacrificing to help others, giving up personal time to be available for those in need, but when you actually see someone like Phyllis serving effortlessly with genuine love, you know you have been in the presence of one of the Lord's special "saints."

I picked up the *Town Talk* newspaper at Shipley's Donuts. There was the article about Joyce coming for the fitness seminar. "F.U.N. Aerobics Combines Methods" was the headline.[11] The interviewer did an excellent job of distinguishing between Bob and Joyce's program and other popular aerobic classes out there; there were no routines to learn, the music was updated often, the program boasted of several exercise levels, and it was low impact and science based. In the photo, she looked beautiful as usual—a gorgeous example of a fit woman over 50 … and me? Oh geez, the camera caught me saying something in mid-sentence with my tongue sticking half out with an awkward expression. Get over myself! Why can't I lose the pride? Front page placement, decently written article, full color photo, nothing immodest ... just a close-up of Joyce and me from the chest up. Great publicity. Just be thankful! Sweet!

Reunited, our little family had a full morning at church then back home to unpack and eat lunch. While the kids were taking their afternoon nap, I went out to the side yard to tackle the sapling that was planted too close to the driveway and scraped my car last night as I drove under the carport to the side door. I found the big pruning shears, bent the little tree down towards the ground and held it there with my foot. I began squeezing the handles hard until the blades were locked around its little trunk. It required more effort than I had estimated, and when I threw more of my body weight into it, I lost my balance and my foot slipped off the trunk base. Whap!! That bent branch whiplashed back upright with such velocity that it slapped right into my forehead and knocked me backwards onto the grass. I sat there a few minutes with my head throbbing and tears of pain rolling down my cheeks. Then I realized that no one was coming to rescue me with kisses and first aid, so I bucked up and went inside to grab a baggy of ice. In the bathroom mirror I got a close-up view to survey the damage. Already a wicked bump was swelling up, and black and blue bruising would soon follow. I would need to wear an aerobic headband tomorrow, but not because it was the raging style.

Naptime was over, then it was playtime, dinnertime, bath time, story time, and bedtime, and all the time was gone. I had to plan for the next day of Monday classes, and school would be starting in a few weeks for Hudson. There was still so much to do to get him ready for first grade. Our Presbyterian church had begun a school named "Grace Christian," and the board had accepted Hudson on a full scholarship. He met both qualifications: he was extremely smart, and we did not have the means to pay for private school. There was **Re-** again. She was shedding God's unmerited favor on us and providing for all our needs.

Monday & Tuesday blitzed by ... private dance therapy for an autistic student, morning and evening aerobics, Pre-School Creative Movement at a daycare center, tumbling classes, and ballet levels I, II, and advanced pointe classes at the YWCA. Oh yeah, I promised Ann I would call the police about my obscene phone caller, but what would THAT look like? What would THAT mean? Would they then come out to the house to take a report and frighten the children? And realistically, what could they really do about the situation? I excused myself with the "I'm too busy today" line, but because I promised Ms. Ann, I determined I would go to the police station Friday afternoon ... right after my ex picked up the children for weekend custody.

When you're a single mom living alone in a house with young children, you can't think about what bad things could happen to you. If you did, you would be paralyzed with fear and anxiety, unable to power through the long days of work and tending to your children's needs for love, care, and security. So, what were my rules for coping?

Rule #1: avoid the newspaper as much as possible—it was best not to know about terrible events. Rule #2: same for TV—catch the weather but skip the news.

My formula seemed to work- I managed to stay upbeat, surrounding myself with positive, wonderful people from my church, my associates at the YWCA, and certification participants. There was no room for weakness, for being a scaredy-cat. I told myself to NOT think about it if my mind wandered down a dark alley.

I never remember being afraid … afraid to go places, to be alone, to travel the highways to Dallas at night. I was fearless. Looking back, I'm sure that was a liability, not an asset. In today's world, it is most assuredly good to have a healthy sense of caution, to recognize your areas of vulnerability and blind spots, and to be aware of your surroundings. My body language and actions unknowingly broadcast a loud message that seemed to say to certain alert opportunists who watch and target victims, "I dare you!" I was probably over-confident, but at the time, I didn't see it that way. I thought I was demonstrating my faith in God to protect me and the children. I thought that there was no way that bad things could happen to good people, and we were "good" people. Was I living with a false sense of security, not grounded in a realistic view of the world? Probably yes.

Our family Bible memorization verse was from the Old Testament book of Proverbs:

"Trust in the Lord with all your heart And do not lean on your own understanding. In all your ways acknowledge Him, And He will make your paths straight.

Do not be wise in your own eyes; Fear the Lord and turn away from evil.

It will be healing to your body And refreshment to your bones"

(Proverbs 3: 5-8).

My little family—the two children and myself—were fearing the Lord and turning away from evil.

Unfortunately, evil doesn't turn away from us:

"Be of sober spirit, be on the alert. Your adversary, the devil, prowls around like a roaring lion, seeking someone to devour" (I Peter 5:8).

Satan is my true enemy—the architect of evil. He is always the opportunist— looking for those moments when our guard is lowered, and he can use his agents to attack—usually at night, under the cover of darkness.

Re- *and* Me

Goodnight!

That Tuesday night after the successful weekend F.U.N. Fitness seminar, I finished teaching at the YW at 9:00 p.m.—it was my late night. On Tuesdays, I had a 45-minute break from the time that after-school care finished until my next two dance classes began. I would take the children over to our grandmotherly, older babysitter's home with their dinner and pajamas in tow. She fed them and got them ready for bed. After I finished teaching, I would go back over to pick them up. The kids were usually asleep when I put them in their car seats. This evening, by the time I got home, darkness covered the sky. There was very little moonlight. Dang! I wish someone could replace the lights on my front porch. The ceiling is way too high for me and my short ladder. From car seat to bed Kid #1, and now Kid #2. Done! Car locked. Front door locked and dead bolted with the key hanging on the wall. Change into my favorite summer comfy night gown. Minimal routine: wash face, brush teeth, collapse in bed. Nighttime Bible reading. Grateful prayers. Made it through another day!

I am WOMAN! I am Strong! (and just in case, I have a big, sharp butcher knife on the shelf above my head).

Chapter 6

ARE YOU THERE?

Darkness. Silence.
How long have I lain here? Patience. Just wait.
Wait longer. How long should I wait?
Do nothing. How long can I do nothing?
I must know ... No! Wait! STOP! I hear something. Be still.
Heart stop beating so loud. Strain to listen.
Footsteps? Yes. Footsteps!
Are they coming back towards me again? Please No!
I can't endure another AGAIN.
The sound. It is getting fainter.
Is that the sound of footsteps walking away from me?
Yes. Away.
Across the carpet. Louder. Not nearer. A different louder.
Footsteps tapping across tile.

Re- *and* Me

Bathroom tile or kitchen tile? A door opening? I'm sure of it.
I'm sure that's a door opening.
Bathroom door nearby? No!
Farther away. Across the kitchen.
My back door. Was that it closing?
SILENCE. Now Nothing. Nothing means nothing.
It could be a trap. The nothing before something again.
Not again!

Don't move. How long can I not move?
My hands. I can't get my mind off my hands.
I can't feel them move anymore.
How many hours have I not felt?
Is it over now? Time is quickly passing.
I must know. Wait. Be sure. Don't move.
My hands are numb. Tingling. They are dead.
I can't be a ballerina with dead hands.
I must move. I must try.

I begin to wiggle forward. Wiggle more. Yes. The bed.
I feel the bottom edge of the bed with my head.
Is that the short side of the bed or the long side?
Keep moving. Keep scooching.
Ow! That burns. It hurts my skin.
Nothing between me and the carpet.
Nothing. No barrier. No protection. No clothing.
Another Ow! Is that my head butting against the baseboard?

Are You There?

I'm disoriented. Stop. Visualize. Think.
Glide your head along the baseboard.
Open space at the end. Shoes.
My closet. My OPEN closet. How did it get open?
Where would my bedroom door be?
Scoot the other way. Another opening.
My door. My OPEN door. Keep wiggling. Keep moving.
Push your feet against the carpet.
Inch by inch. Be an inchworm.

The hallway. I must be in the hallway.
Tuck your legs into a ball. Turn. Stretch them out.
The floor. The tile floor. Yes! The cold bathroom tile floor.
Their door is THIS way. Push with your legs.
Bend-scooch. Bend-scooch.
My head should have hit their door by now. Thud!
The door. It moved. Their OPEN door.
Oh, my Lord! Oh no, Oh no. PLEASE NO!
Their door has been OPEN.
My door has been OPEN. For hours.
How could they not hear? How did they not wake up?
Unless they CAN'T wake up, Lord, No! PLEASE NO!

"Hudson! Hudson!" Silence.
(louder) "HUDSON! Are you there?" Silence again.
"Hudson, can you hear me?" Silence. Darkness.
"Wake up! Please wake up. It's Mommy here."

Wiggle more. Get closer. The room is huge. The ceilings are high. My voice is weak.

God give me strength. Be merciful. *He had a switchblade.*

"HUDSON!" I cried out, "it's Mommy – **ARE YOU THERE?**"

Nothing. Nothing. Then … *something.*

"Yes," said a sleepy little voice, "Mommy is that you?"

Beautiful words. Words of Life.

"Yes, Buddy, it's me. Are you OK?"

"Yes, OK—am OK. Where are you?

I can't see—too dark," he said timidly.

He must have turned all their night lights off.

"I'm right here. On the floor. Inside your door.

I'm going to say our family Bible verse … Proverbs 3:5-6.

You say it with me and follow the path to MY VOICE."

Trust in the Lord with all your heart and do not lean on your own understanding In all your ways acknowledge Him, and He will make your paths straight.

"Here you are! Brave boy! I love you so much! Is your room dark? Are the night lights turned off? Yes?" I assumed as much.

"Now," I instructed him, "don't be frightened. Mommy is hurt and looks bad. I want you to reach up and pull the light switch on. Then, turn away from me and run to Dawn's bed to see if she is OK."

More tired wee voice noises from the other side of the room. My little girl's voice. Thank you, Lord for sparing me a mother's deepest sorrow. Both my children are alive!

"Dawn is awake. I made her awake," said Hudson.

"Dawn. Sweet girl. I love you—love you! Mommy is over here. I need your help. Can you bring *Crunchie* over and share her with me?"

Dawn was my thumb sucker—she still needed that thumb in her mouth for comfort, especially when she rubbed the satin binding on her golden colored blankie she named, *"Crunchie."*

"Don't be scared. Both of you come over here. Lay *Crunchie* over Mommy and cover me up," I told them, trying to be brave myself.

The next thing I knew, I felt *Crunchie's* familiar soft brushed cotton across my body, then two little bodies snuggled up to me. I heard them both crying. "Mommy, Mommy, where are your eyes? Where are your hands?" sobbed Dawn.

"I understand," I whispered to them softly, "Mommy is OK. My eyes are under the tape. My hands are still here behind my back. See?"

I went on, "A bad guy snuck into our house to try and hurt me. But he is gone now. We are safe."

I needed their help so I could get into the kitchen to phone the police. It was a tall order for a six- and four year-old. With both my hands and feet bound it took all my strength to sit against the wall and push up to standing, even with both of my little ones trying to help. Not only that, but my left hip felt weird.

The Good Guys Show Up

"Hudson, you have to help Mommy stand up, so I can hop into the kitchen to the picnic bench. Dawn, you hold *Crunchie* and keep her covering me up as I hop ... we made it," I congratulated them.

"Hudson, we're going to play some games—the first one is 'Simon says;' are you ready?" I asked.

Simon says: *Crawl up on the barstool and turn on the kitchen light.*

Simon says: *Take the phone receiver off the hook.*

"Nice job, Hudson, I can hear the dial tone."

Simon says: *Dial these numbers:* **9-1-1**. *If they ask you if this is an emergency ...*

Simon says: *Say YES!*

"Is that them? Are you talking to them?"

Simon says: *Tell them to get the police. Tell them we've been attacked by a bad guy.*

"OK, OK, Hudson, game over. Good Job. Enough talking. My turn now. Bring the phone over to me so I can talk to the people. Hold the phone up for me," I instructed him.

"Hello? Yes! I've been attacked by a strange man in my home. My address is … - Street.

I'm tied up with ropes, and I can't come to the front door. My six- year-old son will let the officers in.

Yes, I'll stay on the line."

"Dawn, you have to hold the phone up for Mommy. Don't hang it up. Yes! You can talk to the people," I told her. My little *Chatty Cathy* doll baby was happy about that—she loved to talk!

"Hudson, listen to me. Next game. Now you are Superman, and you are going to save us. Got that? Just like when you pretend with your Superman pajamas. Use your super strength to drag the barstool all the way across the living room and push it against the wall next to the front door. GO! Do that now! YELL when you are there. There yet? Can you hear me?" I shouted. "Am I loud enough? Yes? OK, crawl up onto the chair and stand up so you can turn on the light and reach the big key hanging on the wall."

"I got it, Mommy, I got the key!" he shouted triumphantly.

"YOU WON! Climb down and fit the key into the door lock … like Mario Brothers … use the key to unlock the door. Get the princess out. It's a puzzle—keep trying to fit it in."

"Oh, Mommy—lots and lots of red lights. The police cars are here. The policemen are coming up to the door with flashlights," Hudson shouted back to me excitedly.

"Stay right there next to the door," I instructed him firmly, "the 'Good Guys' are going to help us."

"Hello? Yes, my little boy is at the front door," I told the emergency operator on the phone, "the police are here. Tell them that my son has the deadbolt key, but he needs instructions to be able to unlock the door."

"Hi son, what's your name?" the officer said, talking to him through the front window. "I'm Captain Ritchie. Your name is Hudson? Good, Hudson. You have the key in, but you can't open the door?" he confirmed. "OK, Hudson, you look like a smart boy. I'm going to tell you how to turn it, so you can let us inside to help your Mommy," he coached loudly through the window.

The next thing I heard was the front door opening, the voices of several men talking in a reassuring tone to Hudson, then the sound of big footsteps and pattering bare feet moving across the living room hardwood floor onto our kitchen tile.

"Oh my God! My God! LOOK AT HER!" exclaimed one voice.

Look at her? I remember wondering, *and see what? What do I look like?*

Totally exposed: completely naked with Dawn's blankie draped over the front of me but with my backside open. Duct tape wrapped round and round my head covering my eyes and stuck to my hair. My hands behind my back—secured with layers of ropes, tape, and more ropes and tape. My feet bound at my ankles, wrapped around with rope and tied with a long, extended rope for hanging. Oh, and not to forget that huge knot on my forehead where the sapling tree zapped me a few days before. Not a pretty sight.

I heard another officer with a voice of authority quietly direct someone to take the kids into their bedroom. "No! Please wait!" I insisted. "Bring my children close to me, so I can talk to them first." When I felt their little hands on the top of my shoulders as I sat on the picnic bench, I told them, "Mommy is so proud of you two … you have been the bravest children EVER! The policemen are going to help me now … they are going to get the tape off my eyes, so I can see you and cut off the ropes so I can hug you. Can you go to your room and show the officer your toys? Dawn, I need to borrow *Crunchie* for a bit longer, but I promise I will give her right back to you. Love You!" I tried to sound casual and confident.

It wasn't until AFTER they left the kitchen, and I heard their bedroom door close that I started shaking and trembling … my whole body heaved up and down as I inhaled and exhaled rapidly—hyperventilating. I couldn't catch my breath. Oh my gosh! Oh my gosh!

What just happened?

Is it over, are my kids safe?

How did we do that?

How did Hudson call the police, find that key, and fit it in the door to unlock it by himself?

How did Dawn stay so calm next to me?

How did I keep it together long enough to crawl into their room and give them directions?

I truly have no answers. No human explanation anyway.

I believe it could only have been the supernatural **GRACE** of God that enabled us to do all that. It was my little friend, **Re-**, giving me the serenity to **re**group, **re**focus, and **re**gain my composure.

I heard a soothing voice next to my ear, "Ma'am, I'm Captain Ritchie, and we are here to help you. We are so sorry. Your name is Rebecca-is that right? OK, Rebecca, are you hurting anywhere?"

"Yes! Yes, I'm hurting everywhere," I let them know. "But my hands—I'm going to lose my hands. They've been numb for hours-I need to teach, to dance. I can't be a ballerina with no hands. Just get these ropes off."

"We're going to get the ropes and tape off as soon as we can, but we have to do it slowly and carefully," he explained. "We need to get all the evidence we can to nail that S.O.B. who did this to you and put him away!" I sensed a certain righteous anger and indignation in his voice just then … and a determination to defend and protect. I could trust Captain Ritchie.

Another voice came to me quietly in the other ear, "Ma'am, is there a friend who can come pick up the children and take them away to their place? Is there someone you trust who can take care of them during this process?"

"Well, yes," I stammered, "but I can't think, I can't think—I'm blank—I can't think of anybody's name."

"That's normal," said the voice called Captain Ritchie. "You are in shock."

"My church. There are lots of good people at my church. I have friends … I can't remember names," I said, starting to panic. "I know, I know! There's a book—a directory, a church directory. It's in the drawer under the phone. Can you find it? Look in the front pages. There's a list of the leaders, it will say *Elders or Session*. Read them to me."

"I found it," said one of the officers, then he started reading off names of the men on the list: "Dick Ayres, Jack Mertens, Randy. . ."

"Stop! Dick Ayres. You can call him. He will know what to do. Please hurry! Get these ropes off my wrists, now my arms are numb, too," I said with a sense of urgency—no longer calm.

My brain was jumbled. The shock factor was HUGE. I know the police carefully cut off all the ropes and duct tape to finally free my hands and then started on the ones around my ankles, but I still couldn't see. I heard some new voices coming in through the back door—I thought I recognized one voice. I heard the clunk of a metal box slamming the floor. One of the new voices introduced himself to me saying he was a medic with CenLa and would be cutting the tape off from around my head. Yes, his voice did sound familiar, but I wasn't sure. I was confused. I felt a cuff wrapping around my arm. Someone was taking my blood pressure. A cold stethoscope pressed against my chest. They tried to pull the duct tape off from around my head to preserve as much of my hair as possible. I'm not sure if it was worth it. All the tugging and pulling hurt too much. Finally, they just cut my hair to get the last layer of duct tape off. At last, I could open my eyes.

I was mortified at whose face was in front of me. It was one of my ex's good friends from his days as a medic at CenLa. Friends naturally "take sides" when there is a bitter divorce and custody battle, so that pitted him "against" me. I was humiliated for him to see me like this, and I even wondered if secretly he was glad. I never knew. To his credit, outwardly, he stayed professional and courteous.

I looked on the picnic table. There, I saw the ropes and tape, still with bunches of my hair stuck to it. They were logged into various evidence bags. The medics gave me blankets to cover up so I would be able to give *Crunchie* back to Dawn. Dick Ayres eventually arrived and packed some clothes and toys for the kids. I got to finally hug them good-bye, and I told them I would come see them later. Dick said he was taking them over to his daughter's home where my children had played before. They would be safe and cared for. I knew they were traumatized as well.

While the medics were finishing up what could be done for me there, I was told I needed to get a ride to Saint Frances Cabrini Hospital where they had just inaugurated the new "Rape Crisis Center." The officers asked me what woman friend could I call to help me and drive me there? I had memorized the number of my fellow English teacher friend, Anita, and amazingly could recall it. I also had them look up Ms. Masden's home phone number and call her as well. She told them she would meet us at the hospital.

While we were waiting for my friend Anita to arrive, the police asked me basic questions: my attacker's description, the timeline, what he said to me, and the sequence of events. I rattled off information in a detached sort of way, as if I was describing the plotline of a novel that I had just read ... not like I was telling them about the vicious rape I just survived. I told them I distinctly remember the intruder's footsteps going across my kitchen floor and the sound of the back door opening and closing and then it was silent for a long time, and he didn't come back. They said that wasn't possible; the front and back doors were both locked securely with the deadbolt key. I insisted that I distinctly remember his exit.

I don't remember anything about how I got dressed, got into Anita's car, or the trip to the hospital. As a dancer, I'm a very visual creature, so it's strange to me how some memories are so vividly clear and how others elude me. I do have a picture of Anita driving into the parking lot right in front of the Emergency Entrance to the hospital. I was comforted to see my "Steel Magnolia," Ms. Masden, sitting in her car waiting for me. I needed from her the gift of that rare flower ... both her strength and her softness ... to get me through the days ahead. Before opening the door, I paused a moment to look out the car window at the first rays of the sun coming up. I realized it was dawn. Morning time and mourning time ... Wednesday morning, August 19, 1987—an unwanted anniversary date.

The attack covered a relatively short time span of 4 hours or so.

The repercussions of the rape have affected me for a lifetime.

One short night for the rapist. One long, never-ending nightmare for the victim.

Chapter 7

THE DOCTORS

Condemnation-Examination

I WAS TAKEN to Saint Frances Cabrini Hospital—a private Catholic Hospital in backwards Central Louisiana, and yet they had the most innovative and progressive program available at the time: rape kits and trained medical personnel to administer the kits. How was this possible? The DNA typing method was first used in casework in the United Kingdom in 1985 and then in commercial laboratories in the USA in late 1986, but the method was not adopted by the FBI until 1988.[12] Yet, in August of 1987, the Rape Crises Center in Alexandria was on the cutting edge of technology for processing sexual assault victims.

Ann and Anita sat beside me on the plastic chairs in the hospital hallway of the ER while I filled out the patient profile forms. The nurse came to get the clipboard from me and literally led me with her arm around my shoulder into the examination room where she had me sit on the edge of the table … the lights were especially bright.

The attending doctor rather burst into the room with a high level of enthusiasm almost as bright as the lights, grabbed the clipboard off the desk and glanced over it. He then turned to face me as he introduced himself and attempted to pronounce my last name, "Rebecca…Rebecca XXXX", he said.

"Rebecca **XXXX**" I corrected him with some sense of control over my name anyway.

"Hmm. Sounds familiar. Where would I have seen your name lately?"

"Maybe," I stammered, "in the Sunday paper; my picture was there with an article about my fitness business."

"That's it! Well, well," the doctor said with what seemed like a knowing chuckle, "I guess somebody ELSE saw your picture in the paper and liked it!"

Inside my head I was thinking, "What did he just say? Is he saying because my photo was in the newspaper, that I'm somehow responsible for being targeted as a rape victim? Is that the connection?" I was speechless. I just sat there like a scolded child in the principal's office pressured to play the scapegoat and admit that everything was my fault. I really didn't need that stab in my "guilty" gut right now. I wish I could say that this insensitive doctor was the only guy who acted like a jerk by insinuating that I deserved THIS (rape) because _____ (fill in the blank). Unfortunately, his comments were only the first of many gut punches to come.

    The nurse came up to my side right away, perhaps sensing the offense, and began to explain what was about to happen to me. They would start collecting the forensic evidence needed to hopefully find my attacker. Inside, I was thrown into panic mode again—my heart racing and my ears were resounding with the words, "I can't do this, I can't do this," over and over—so I couldn't hear exactly what she was saying … or I didn't want to hear. My legs were weak and wobbly as they stood me up and spread a special white sheet across the examination table. I just closed my eyes, and silent tears started rolling down my cheeks as she lay me back down onto the table and extended the bottom half to support my legs. A high intensity operating light was lowered down over me.

    A flashlight … the rapist used a flashlight! The surgical light triggered a memory of my attacker shining a light up and down my body "examining me" while he made comments. There was a small gap in the tape under one of my eyes that would capture the light as it passed over me—coming and going like headlights from passing cars on the highway.

    The whole experience of gathering evidence is humiliating—even degrading, dehumanizing, as they swab every part of your body inside and out, comb through your hair … ALL of your hair … slowly and meticulously with fine toothed combs, and scrape under every nail while you try to lie still and contain yourself.

It was a **re-raping**! I felt victimized all over. It was invasive—horrible. It was a traumatic but needed necessity—I was assured by the nurse during the tedious process. But no amount of pseudo-soothing words could alleviate the excruciating emotional pain of having to be touched again in this manner in the raw vulnerable hours following an attack.

Any girl or woman who submits herself to undergo a Rape Kit Examination for DNA evidence should be recognized as a true heroine. Her bravery, as contrasted to the cowardness of her attacker, gives law enforcement, juries, and judges crucial incriminating evidence that can lock him away and save other women from the trauma of being sexually assaulted. It is worth it, but the sacrifice a victim makes to endure the forensic exam does not come without a price. To this day, even decades later, I cannot undergo a probing examination by a male dermatologist for my annual skin cancer check. Neither can I be a patient of a male physician in the OB/GYN specialty. Even with a female practitioner, those "silent tears" of a painful memory will still flow down my cheeks during a pelvic exam.

Once the forensic exam was complete and the kit was sealed to send off to the labs in Shreveport, the doctor began his physical exam of me to check for injuries. The circulation had returned to my hands once the ropes and tape had been cut off, but my right hand was still numb and tingly. The numbness in my hand and in my heart were the same—dead, empty, non-feeling. He said that my hand should heal up with time, that the nerves were probably compressed and damaged, but should regenerate ... key word being "should." Today, I still have numbness in that right hand and find it difficult to hold a pen and write nicely. When I cycle outdoors, leaning on the handlebars, I constantly need to shake out my right hand to get circulation back into the fingers. These were minor injuries of small consequence.

Not so minor is what happened to my left hip. During the ordeal, the rapist would force his whole body up between my legs which were tied together at the ankles. As my hips were forced and crammed open, the muscles of my buttock just popped and detached off the bone. Instead of my gluteal being "rounded" and curving "out" because that muscle is tight onto the bone, it indented inward. Dr. Bob Ward said he had seen this type of injury in quarterbacks when the biceps of their throwing arm would detach off the arm bone from the force constantly placed on them. I'm sure if I had been an NFL player making the big bucks ($$$), I could have had surgery to reattach it properly, but single moms with only "catastrophic" insurance just have to keep going, and eventually, it did grow back and reattach *somehow*. But the *somehow* caused me problems later. The biomechanics of my left hip joint were compromised and thus began the long process of osteoarthritis deterioration leading to a left hip replacement at a relatively young age and later also the right hip because of all the years of imbalance from the initial injury to the other hip. God's design of the human body is so brilliant and beautifully balanced that any small deviations in that perfect alignment will eventually lead to disfunction and a chronic injury.

Dr. "Done"

After the forensic and physical exams, I asked the doctor of the Rape Crises Center if I was now going to have a D&C (dilation and curettage) procedure or shot or something to prevent pregnancy. The doctor said, "Nope, that's not protocol for a Catholic Hospital, and all we do here is the rape exam. You will need to make an appointment with your own OB/GYN this morning for any other procedures that you think are necessary."

BAM! I felt like someone just dropped me off a cliff. I hit bottom hard. I endured that invasive examination. Your professional responsibility is done, and now you tell me I'm on my own? "Good-bye! Oh, and good luck with not getting pregnant, AIDS, STDs, and finding some counseling." Now I was truly in a "rape crises"!

I'm guessing that the center was in the earliest stages of concept development, and looking back more objectively, I'm glad they got ONE of the most important things right: collection of DNA evidence.

I finally came out of the examination room and found Ms. Ann and Anita still at their posts waiting for me. What time was it? Around 7:30 a.m.? I had no sense of time.

I described some of what happened behind those closed doors. I told them what the doctor said back to me when I told him he probably recognized my name from the newspaper. Ann was furious! I'm not sure, but I think she might have walked back to that room to talk to that doctor … if not right then, I'm sure she didn't let that insult go unanswered. Ms. Ann was all about the "**W**" of "Y**W**CA;" she was an outspoken advocate for women's rights and treatment.

We used the pay phone at the hospital to call my OB/GYN office when it opened at 8:00 a.m. I had a hard time getting out the words and sequencing of events for the receptionist; I could hardly verbalize what had happened to me, but I explained to her that I was a victim of a stranger rape. l had completed the forensic exam at the Rape Crises Center, but they told me to go to my own OB/GYN for the rest of the treatments I would need. Yes, I could come right away and wait to get into him, but please tell him and the nurses what happened to me—I don't want anyone in the waiting room to overhear me when I sign in.

Ann had to leave from the hospital to go home and get ready for work at the "YW," but Anita didn't have to be back in her classroom for a few more weeks, so she said she would stay with me and drive me to my doctor's office. I sat in her car in silence all the way to the office, but I did manage to take a deep breath and come to a place of gratefulness for the people God had put in my life.

*When I said earlier that the people in Alexandria were "that good," I was only beginning to discover just how good ... and selfless, and caring, and giving they were. My Little 2-Letter Friend, **Re-**, God's **grace**, was everywhere. She was working through people and circumstances and surrounding me with supernatural, sustaining strength. The ordinary congregation members at my church, the leaders and pastor, the staff at the YWCA, caring Christian people in the community I'd never even met before ... all helped and assisted me in extraordinary ways. They were the "hands and feet of Jesus," holding me and walking with me through this dark valley that felt like a death of sorts.*

Dr. "Don't Know"

I arrived at the office of the huge OB/GYN practice with multiple doctors in partnership and signed in. It all looked familiar—the same spacious waiting room where I came for my prenatal check-ups before Dawn's birth. The receptionist finally called my name and I went up to check in. Insurance card? Not for an office visit. Pre-payment? Nope! Got nothing. Somehow, I was escorted back to an examination room.

Eventually, my doctor came into the room with his nurse and nonchalantly asked what he could do for me. "Why are you here today ... what's the reason for your visit?" he casually questioned, while looking down at his clipboard as he scribbled notes.

"Why am I here today?!!! (Question mark followed by GIANT Exclamation marks.) You really don't know?" I answered in disbelief. "I called ahead and explained everything to the receptionist. She was supposed to fill you in privately on my circumstances before I got here. So then, you don't even know what has happened to me?" I exclaimed in desperation. "A stranger broke into my home last night. **I'm a rape victim!**" I put it bluntly.

THAT got his attention! He turned to his nurse with both a surprised and an annoyed look, perhaps blaming her for the embarrassment of catching him off guard. He directed his nurse to immediately escort me to his office for a private consultation. I felt small and powerless, seated in the light framed chair in front of his oversized executive desk. As he nervously swiveled back and forth in his cushy chair, I briefed him on the rape and subsequent examination at the "Catholic" Cabrini Hospital's Rape Crises Center. I told him that Dr. "Done" there told me to go to my own doctor to discuss any concerns I might have. How about pregnancy for starters? I explained my reality to my OB/GYN:

> *"Sir, I'm a single mom of two young children, making my living teaching dance and fitness. I have handled situations you probably can't imagine since becoming a single parent, but I'm not sure I can cope with having a rapist's baby right now ... not being able to work and support my children plus adding another baby. I'm a Christian*

woman of faith, so I will never abort a baby. I need you to give me a shot or whatever doctors do to PREVENT conception after a rape. To answer your original question, THAT is why I'm here today!"

My OB/GYN looked uncomfortable delivering his personal stance on the subject under these circumstances and stammered, "I am sorry, but no, I can't help you ... I'm Catholic too, and I took an oath as a physician in that faith to preserve life, so I can't give you a shot or any procedure that would prevent conception."

"What!" I exclaimed incredulously. "Are there no exceptions for rape? You don't understand. I don't want to end life either, but you could interrupt the conception process before it happens!"

Well, my doctor could do that ... he had the scientific knowledge and medical permission to act on that knowledge, but not the personal *moral* permission to help me in my situation. There must be another way ...

"OK, then what about the other doctors in this practice? If you morally can't compromise your oath, I respect that, but please check to see if one of your partners isn't Catholic and could help me." I made my case and then he actually got out from behind his desk and said, "I don't really know. I will go check with them."

You don't really know? You have been professional partners with these men for years and you don't even know their faith, if they have one, and yet in your profession it affects the whole future of a patient like me? Ten minutes later he returned and told me apologetically, "No, I checked with my other two partners, they also are Catholic and took the same pledge and vow."

I was beginning to crumble, "I know there are more than three doctors in this group," I suggested. "Surely there is a protestant somewhere in this practice … in this town! Please, go check and see if any of the other doctors can sign off on this." Dr. "Don't Know" could see I was reaching a breaking point, so he left the office again. This time he returned with a smile on his face which seemed at odds with our subject matter, and jubilantly said, "Yes! Dr. 'W' will authorize his nurse to treat you."

I expressed how grateful I was for his efforts to help me, while not compromising his own convictions. In my own head though, I was struggling with this "Catholic" line of reasoning. I was only wanting to prevent conception, so there was no pregnancy—how could that be wrong?

We were talking **Emergency Conception** *procedures here, not giving me a medication or procedure that would have an abortifacient effect of terminating an existing pregnancy. I've since learned that even in 2020, there is still debate within Catholic medical facilities concerning their stance on allowable procedures in the case of an unjust rape. More ethics experts and Catholic Bishops are leaning toward the permission to provide Emergency Contraception aka … the "morning-after pill" or a hormone shot, provided that tests are made to* *confirm that there is no existing pregnancy that would be aborted. There is usually a 72-hour window of time to make this decision.*[13]

At this point and time in history, and for his own conscience sake just to rule out the possibility of an existing pregnancy before the rape, my doctor asked personal questions about my "sex life." Was there was any chance at all that I could be pregnant from a prior relationship because then, the shot the nurse would give me would cause an abortion. "Zero, nada, none!" I guaranteed him. "I haven't dated or been with a man in any intimate way for two years since my separation and divorce … just taking care of my kids, working, and serving."

I wasn't sure exactly what was in the "morning-after" shot—some combination of hormones that act by suppressing ovulation or disrupting fertilization, but it wasn't so bad. However, the nurse said these next shots would be bad. She would need to give me two HUGE penicillin shots in each buttock to prevent STDs (Sexually Transmitted Diseases). I had managed to make it through the entire night of the rape in silence but for the first time, I screamed loudly. Indeed, the shots were agonizing—slow going in and ever so painful … Again, it felt like a **re-rape**! I was told that a future AIDS infection was something I also needed to consider. I would need to be tested every year for the next seven to ten years to see if I had contracted the virus and needed treatments because it can lay dormant and show up later. Oh great!

The Doctors

It was incredulous to me how one traumatic event in my life that occurred over a several hour time span could reach far into my future and affect me in a multitude of ways for decades to come.

Chapter 8

A QUIET PLACE

Wednesday. Midmorning.
What now? Where to?
Wonderful people were at work while I sat in
Waiting rooms . . .

DICK AYRES CAME to pick me up. He had arranged a safe place for me to recuperate. I would stay in the home of a couple from our church, parents with school-age children. They were a busy family like everyone else but were willing to open their house and hearts to me. Mr. Ayres thought it would be good for us to first drop by his daughter's home and check in on my kids, to let them know that I was OK. It was a celebratory moment to be able to drive up and see my children running out to the car to greet me—happy, safe, and alive. I could see that they were having a great time at their place. I knew then that I could give myself permission to take the "luxury" of some more time away from them to nurse my wounds. I needed to get into a better place emotionally, to be able to pick them up the next day and take them back to the scene of the crime, our home.

My host, Betsy, was welcoming and had lunch waiting for me. Everything I did was surreal—putting a napkin in my lap, picking up a spoon to eat soup … normal everyday activities seemed foreign to me now—I had changed; life had changed in one terrible 12-hour period. Betsy's husband was an executive for Avon, and even though it was August, their den was filled with a cheerful Christmas display of products for their distributors to come by and view. Christmas. Happiness. I felt "hollow." Would I ever be filled with joy again? Could Jesus bring healing and peace back into my life? Was God's grace, my friend **Re**-, enough to **re**store me to a semblance of the person I was yesterday? Today it seemed **re**mote.

Mamoo

After lunch, Betsy asked if I had already talked with my relatives back in Dallas. I had. Anita insisted I let my dad know what had happened to me. NO WAY would I ever call my grandmother, "Mamoo," and tell her what just happened! How many times did she lecture me growing up? *"Lock your car doors; hold your purse with both hands to the outside away from people passing you; put a chain lock on your door, etc."* I didn't need any guilt trips from her such as: "*This was your fault. You could have prevented it if you had just locked your doors properly like I told you to do.*" I believed that in some way I failed them. I didn't protect myself and the children. Surely, I must be responsible for the rapist being able to get into my house.

"Mamoo" was our childhood nickname for my paternal grandmother. My father was an only child, so we were her only four very spoiled grandchildren. She viewed us as an "extension" of herself rather than the separate and unique individuals that we were who believed differently from her. You could NEVER tell her that. She was kind and loving but the most stubborn, opinionated, and dominant person I have ever known. In all my life, she never admitted once, not even once, that she was wrong about anything. She would always manage to twist words, actions, and experiences around so that she always came out "right." Arguing with her was futile. My mother, Beth, was never a good enough wife for her son and not a proper housekeeper or mother. I have my own theories for why she acted this way … grew up in the country, poor, eloped with the rich and powerful boss's son at age 16, never finished high school, thrown into higher society life, lived through the Great Depression—so in my opinion, she was extremely insecure and overcompensated her perceived inadequacies by dominating people. All theories aside, she was a force to be reckoned with and in NO uncertain terms, I begged my dad to not let Mamoo talk him into driving here. I was well taken care of, and I was not ready to be forced to deal with her criticisms.

Re- *and* Me

Where Were My Guardian Angels . . . Off Duty??

Betsy showed me the blurb from the Wednesday morning edition of the *Town Talk* local newspaper:

> "A woman was raped by an intruder in her home near the so-called Garden District early Wednesday morning, according to police Capt. George Fuller. 'A man armed with a knife broke into her house and assaulted and raped the young woman, who reported the incident at 3:08 a.m.' The woman suffered minor physical injuries. He said, 'a couple of small kids were in the house' when the rape occurred, but no information was released regarding what the children might have observed. 'The victim was in bed sleeping when the rapist approached her,' Fuller said."[14]

I needed to call my ex. He would have custody of the kids this coming weekend, and he should know and be prepared for their post-traumatic stress disordered behavior. The conversation did NOT go well. I explained it was a criminal stranger rape, not some "boyfriend" over for the evening, as he insinuated! I had assumed his friends at CenLa Ambulance who took my emergency call had already told him about my attack. What I didn't tell him was that because of some of the things the rapist said to me during the attack and because of the vindictive actions perpetuated by my ex during our separation, divorce, and custody battles, the police had him at the top of their suspect list in a "rape for hire" scenario.

Betsy and I were about the same size, so she provided me with comfortable lounging clothes, a robe, and then some toiletries and fresh towels as she showed me to her lovely bathroom. Up to now, I had not seen myself in a mirror. I closed and locked the bathroom door. This was my first time to be alone with myself to assess the damage done. Some bruises, rope burns, chopped off hair, and then my weird looking left hip muscle that collapsed inwards. Truly, my physical injuries from the attack were considered "minor"—but the psychological wounds were not. I would be dealing with those for years to come.

Oh, and then there was the *spiritual* damage ... just where was God during all this? I thought He was my wall of protection. I believed we were untouchable, surrounded by His guardian angels. I trusted Him ... He had been there for me during ALL the trials and tribulations after my **re**birth salvation experience and ongoing transformation into **Re**-Becky. How could He allow this to happen to me? Were He and my guardian angels on vacation last night? I couldn't wrap my head around this—it felt like a betrayal. Was I abandoned by God?

ReView

The Lord Jesus is my Savior, my **Re**deemer, my Friend. It was His "footprints in the sand" as He carried me when those trials were almost too much to bear. By God's gift of **Grace**, my friend **Re-** right there by me, Jesus has delivered me from "various trials:"

> *"Consider it all joy, my brethren, when you encounter various trials ... " (James 1:2).*

ReMember

I need to **re**call some of the "various trials" God has carried me through these past few years:

1. Through the murky waters of the legal processes as defendant in the separation, custody rulings, property settlement, and final divorce judgment.
2. Through the experiences of being homeless, jobless, and penniless.
3. Through the agonizing and bitter custody battle starting with no custody rights, then given Joint Custody, then awarded Full Custody.
4. Through one after another false child abuse cases filed against me "anonymously" by either my ex or friends of my ex…each one involving surprise visits from the case worker, interviews with my friends and co-workers, private isolated interviews with each child over several stressful months until I received the "Case Closed" letter from Child Protection Services that always arrived, but at the end of the ordeal.
5. Through the most bizarre "trial" that resulted in an

actual court trial date set for my conviction. How could I ever forget the Lord delivering me from that?

*It was the summer of 1986. I had completed the spring semester as a permanent substitute at Peabody Magnet High School for an English teacher who had terminal cancer. This was how I came to be good friends with Anita, the other English teacher next door to me. I was living in the tiny duplex down the street from Owl Grocery and had joint custody of the children by now. I had just started teaching aerobics and dance at the YWCA, and once more, Ms. Ann was looking out for me. She directed me to interview with the Director of the Rapides Parish Schools, "Summer Arts Break," a three-week enrichment camp in July for elementary school children. I got the job and developed the curriculum for my "M.A.D.E. by Rebecca" program (**M**ovement **A**nd **D**ance Education).*

At the end of camp on a hot day in July, the parents were invited to a closing performance. Throughout the morning, each group performed before their family, demonstrating the ballet barre and dance movements they had learned. The last group was almost finished with their presentation when I noticed the back door of the gymnasium open, and two uniformed policemen walked in. They waited for the clapping to die down as the children went into the audience to reunite with their parents. The policemen came up to me, pulled me away from the crowd, announced that they had a warrant for my arrest for threatening to murder a certain "Phyllis XXXX," my husband's current girlfriend whom I had never called, spoken to, or met. They "read me my rights," and one officer pulled my hands behind my back and handcuffed me as the other officer grabbed my purse, which carried my car keys, wallet, and driver's license. To the astonishment of the crying children with their parents still lingering in the gym, they paraded me across to the back door—dressed only in my ballet outfit—leotard, tights, chiffon ballet skirt, and slippers. The uncle of Heather, my young protégé from my YWCA classes who was assisting me, grabbed my sweater, gave it to the officer and then told me that he would gather up the rest of my things to put in his car and meet me at the police station.

Bewildered and humiliated, I walked outside towards the squad car with an officer on each side holding my arms. I looked over the roof of the car to the side street across from the school and really could not believe what I saw. A CenLa Ambulance truck was parked with the medic crew sitting in the front seat watching the whole arrest thing go down. From that distance, I couldn't make out the identities of the medics who were watching me, but I had a pretty good idea ... mostly likely my husband and his partner—or maybe just his partners "spying" out the scene for him. The timing wasn't coincidental ... how did the police know the exact place I would be, and precisely the time of the end of the last performance? And why would a CenLa Ambulance be parked close enough to watch the school but far enough away that they might not have been noticed??

The officers were polite enough and maybe a bit contrite—apologizing as they loaded me in the screened off back seat of the squad car and told me, "Sorry about this Ma'am—we are just *following orders." Maybe they even questioned the absurdity of my criminal arrest. They drove me down to the police station where I was booked. The crime I was accused of—threatening to murder the girlfriend I never knew—was a felony. I was processed through the system, complete with fingerprinting, mugshot, bail set, and a lock-up in the holding cell for several hours ... still in my flimsy ballerina outfit and slippers. Thank goodness for the sweater!*

Fortunately, I was rescued by Heather's Uncle B., who came to the police station, posted my bail, which wasn't cheap, and got me out of jail. The clerk at the police station returned my belongings—my purse and car keys were in a sealed bag with my name on it. Uncle B and Heather guided me out to their car in the parking lot, and he drove me back over to the school where I could pick up my car. He insisted I follow him back over to his home to transfer the stereo and other items he had packed up for me from the school, and to come inside for some tea and biscuits.

I had been to his home many times before, listening to Heather play the piano and chatting about dance and the arts. Heather's mother was a drug addict in New Orleans, and Uncle B., who was her great uncle, had accepted guardianship of her. I had trained her several years before when I was teaching at a local studio, and she followed me when I started teaching ballet again at the YWCA. I took a special interest in her, as she had all the gifts to become a professional ballet dancer: the passion and desire, an expressive movement quality, beautifully arched feet, long lean limber body, an exquisitely beautiful face, and a sweet, teachable disposition. I felt I could help her achieve her goal. Her great uncle, older and retired from school teaching, kept a close watch over Heather—her schooling, her dance training, her diet, her skin care, her friends, and her wardrobe. It was an unusual situation, but we all got along and had become close friends. I was extremely grateful for his generosity in posting my bail and getting me out of that cell none too soon.

From his kitchen phone I called Pastor Bob and asked if I could come over to the parsonage and visit with him after I left Uncle B and Heather. Bob and his wife Sandy knew all about the "bad" Ms. Phyllis (as opposed to my best friend, the "good" Ms. Phyllis). The wicked Phyllis and her husband were former members of the church. Evidently, she had a volatile personality and had pulled all sorts of absurd stunts during her divorce, so she was also known as the "crazy" Ms. Phyllis. Pastor Bob advised me to get in touch with my defense lawyer as soon as possible; if convicted, I was looking at prison time. My trial date was set up for the second week in October, and I would need to mount a solid defense. There could not possibly be a shred of true evidence against me, but somehow in the good ole' boy network here, some crooked judge, lawyer, officials, officers … I never knew who, must have been paid off, paid back, or couldn't tell a lie from the back of their hand.

Regardless of the injustice of it all, my divorce lawyer, Vivian, explained to me that I had to fight this through the flawed justice system. I had to hire and pay her to represent me on this criminal case, subpoena all my phone records, get sworn statements from friends who can testify as to my non-violent character, build a timeline to show my whereabouts on the dates of my supposed threats, etc. All this took time, energy, money (I had to borrow from family), and peace of mind out of me. Vivian told me that when we went to trial and won, then we could ask the judge to order the prosecution to pay for all my legal expenses and compensate me for the "frivolous litigation." Sometime in September, I heard a rumor that my husband and the "bad" Ms. Phyllis had a breakup.

It was two weeks out from the October trial, and all the pieces of evidence for my defense were in place. I was coached and prepped by my lawyer for the questioning phase of the prosecution. Unexpectedly, Vivian called me with the "good news," and I didn't quite know what to say. Evidently since the "bad" Ms. Phyllis and my husband were no longer together, she lost her motivation and decided to drop her case against me. Just like that! It left me holding the financial bag with no recourse for reimbursement. I couldn't countersue for court costs if I didn't go to court, right?

"God Redeems All He Allows" *is a popular quote by Dr. Jim Denison, founder of Denison Ministries.*[15] *It is another way of stating the working principle in one of my favorite Bible verses, "God causes all things to work together for good ... " (Romans 8:28). So then, what "good" did God redeem out of this twisted situation with the "bad" Ms. Phyllis, her relationship with my husband, and her fabricated story of my murderous threats towards her that led to my arrest, short incarceration, and impending trial? I'm still waiting to ask God about a lot of that*

... *but one huge "good" that came out of it was that by default, I **re**ceived full custody of my children. My husband voluntarily **re**turned the children to me just hours after he had picked them up for one of his visitation weekends. Soon thereafter, he and Ms. Phyllis left for a trip to Disney World, I was told, and consequently gave up the rights to his scheduled visitations. I was able to file a change of custody ruling, which was granted.*

Lord, I'm still here sitting on the edge of the bathtub at Betsy's house while the hot water is filling the tub, but where are You? I'm having trouble finding You in this most recent monumental trial. Weren't all the other trials You put me through enough? This one feels like the final crushing blow … I don't know if I can get up again after this one. Your Word says to "*count it all joy when I encounter various trials, knowing that the testing of my faith produces endurance.*" Just how much more endurance do You need to produce in me?

Aren't those court cases, custody cases, child abuse cases, and the felony case enough testing? How much more suffering do You want me to go through? What does the rest of James 1:2–4 say to me?

"And let endurance have its perfect result, that you may be perfect and complete, lacking in nothing".

You want me to grow in **Grace**, to be complete, perfect like Jesus. So … You have allowed these events in my life? And … You will **re**deem all You allow? But when? In the end? At the end? At the end of my life? At the end of time?

Trust You? That's what You are asking of me now? This is my life, the life that You gave back to me. This is my story, the story that You have given me. Give me the courage to tell it and make it count for Your glory.

My conversation alone with God in that bathroom ... affirming the truth and **Re**viewing all the "facts" went something like this:

Dear Heavenly Father,

*I have been saved by Your **grace** alone, and there is no other reason for me to even still be alive. You **re**deemed my life from the pit I had dug for myself and **re**stored my life and my children to me.*

*All I am now is the result of Your gift of salvation, provided by the sacrifice of Your Son, Jesus Christ. He paid the ransom price with His righteous life and blood to **re**deem me.*

I have been given, and I accepted this undeserved gift of eternal life into Your heavenly kingdom.

I understand this with my mind and believe with my heart this to be true.

In Your Word, the Bible, I read that You have saved me for Your purposes I am yet to accomplish.

You have a "good plan for my life," but how can this rape possibly be part of Your "good" plan?

I thank You that you have honored me by allowing me to be tested by all these various trials so that You can show Yourself strong in me,

But honestly, I've had enough. I'm tired. I'm exhausted from trying to "be strong and courageous."

I just can't do it anymore.

I surrender to You and Your will once more.

*If You don't send my friend **Re-** to tightly hold my hand and pull me through this, I don't think I will be able to **re**cover. In my mind I know that:*

> "You are the Lord and there is no other. Besides You there is no God. (verse 5)
>
> You are the one forming light and creating darkness. Causing well-being and creating calamity.

You are the Lord who does all these. (verse 7)

And there is no other God besides You, a righteous God and a Savior" (verse 21)

(Isaiah 45:5,7,21—personalized paraphrase).

My God, I need your healing for my body, for my emotions, for my wounded spirit.

AMEN! *(and that is all I got!)*

No pep rally was at the end of this prayer . . .

No "Remember the Titans—now go out there and win!"

No "I am woman; I am strong!"

Just the cold reality in the warm bath water of my human limits, my weaknesses, my limitations.

Knock-Knock! Who's There?

Some sleep did happen that first night amid fears and the pain from the penicillin shots. In all the aftermath from the attack, exhaustion won out. Faithfully, the hot bright August sun rose the next morning, unaware of my dark clouds. Coffee, breakfast, and a newspaper were provided by my hosts. Another, more descriptive article about my rape and its possible connections to previous rapes was in the *Town Talk*.

There was a phone call from the police—I guess they knew about my "Quiet Place." Oh, they needed me to meet the detectives on my case at my house at 4:00 p.m. for a complete interview and to complete an FBI questionnaire to profile the rapist. With my hosts, I had normal polite conversations about children, church, and then time to just regroup and try to "be." All was peaceful and well until there was a knock at Betsy's door around 2:00 p.m. I was in the kitchen, listening, when I recognized the voices at the front door … my dad and Mamoo!

Obviously, they must have been invited into the living room and then Betsy came into the kitchen to tell me what I already knew … my family was here and wanted to see me.

It was a terrible moment. There was no way I wanted to see my dad and grandmother. Why didn't they respect my wishes? I was a 34-year-old adult, not their little baby girl anymore.

I was infuriated that my dad caved into his controlling mother and allowed her to talk him into making the drive to Alexandria, totally against my explicit wishes … but what did I expect? Hardly anyone could say no or argue with my grandmother. It was totally a foreign idea to them that I could possibly be doing "OK" with my spiritual faith family and not need my biological family at this moment. As I sat stiffly across from them in Betsy's living room, I assured them I would be alright and that I was not ready to talk to them. I knew they probably meant well and that they could not possibly understand how my church family could take such good care of me. They told me the name of the motel they were going to check into and that they would stay there the next few days if I needed them.

I'm scum! More guilt because I was refusing the misdirected help from my own family.

So be it. I couldn't deal with it then.

I needed to get dressed and get someone to take me to the house to meet with the detectives.

Then, I had to get into my own car, pick up the children, and take them home.

I could barely put one foot in front of the other. How would I do this?

My little friend **Re-**, where are you now? Send in for **re**inforcements!

Chapter 9

THE PROFILER

I NEVER SAW my house taped off with yellow "Crime Scene Investigation" barriers with multiple police cars parked in front and detectives inside combing through every room of my home for evidence as others walked the parameter checking the windows, bushes, and yard for clues. My next-door neighbor and friend, Peggy, later described the chaotic scene for me—complete with a crowd of curious gawking neighbors. I am thankful I was spared that further intrusion into what used to be my private life. By the time Betsy drove me over there Thursday afternoon, everything looked "normal" from a curbside view. We sat in the car for a long moment. Before I opened the car door to head up the sidewalk, she asked if she could pray for me and the children … for the Lord to take away the fear and replace it with His peace. I accepted her offer, and

Re- *and* Me

afterwards she placed a new set of house keys in my hand, and we walked up together to try them out in the front door.

My living room smelled of lemon wood polish—the furniture and floors shined. The kitchen was also spic and span; dirty dishes all washed and put away from Tuesday night. The indoor picnic table where I had sat with Dawn waiting for the police to arrive was cleared—no more baggies of tape and ropes. Betsy held my hand as we walked into my bedroom ... it looked like a beautiful picture out of a magazine. New curtains covered my windows, fresh sheets and bedspread were neatly tucked in, 5-star hotel style. The papers and training materials on my makeshift office desk were all organized and stacked, my closet likewise was in order. I had the same experience when I went into the children's bedroom—beds made, all their books and toys on the shelves, and no dirty clothes on the floor.

While I had been resting and recovering over at Betsy's, a team of women from my church, headed by the "good" Ms. Phyllis, had been busy at my house once the police removed the crime scene tape. They purchased real curtains for my bedroom, washed all our dirty clothes and dishes, polished the floors and furniture and made the house as warm and welcoming as they could. Some men from the church had also come over and replaced my locks, fixed the windows that didn't catch and lock properly, and changed the high front porch light I could never reach. I hugged Betsy warmly—a woman I had barely known the day before—but who made herself available for me during this crucial time in my life. "Love your neighbor as yourself" (Mark 12:31) were the words out of the Bible that flashed through my mind as she left. She did that for me.

The Policemen

At 4:00 p.m. precisely, the doorbell rang, and I opened the door to find three policemen—Captain John Ritchie, Detective Tommy Cicardo, and one other officer, who introduced themselves to me. Yes! Three **men**! I'm not even sure if back then there were women police officers or detectives in the department, but today, there was only testosterone. It was awkward. It was intimidating, and as a woman, I felt completely exposed, unprepared, and vulnerable. There was no advocate to emotionally support me as a woman victim. The captain and detective sat squashed together on my grandmother's loveseat, facing me, and the third bigger guy was seated next to them in the comfy Spanish saddle shaped green velvet chair. I sat in my grandmother's straight back chair with the needlepoint cushion, right in the middle of the room facing them with the coffee table between us. I could have used a cup of strong Community coffee right then.

They had their clipboards in their laps and wrote down notes as they interviewed me … now that I think back, I feel certain they must have brought in a portable tape player to record our conversation, but I was so nervous that I could hardly lift my head up to look at them while I spoke, much less take in the details of what they brought in with them.

Re- *and* Me

Captain Ritchie started off by reiterating again how sorry they were for the reason why they were here—the tragedy I was going through. He pledged that he and all the staff at the police department would do everything they could to bring my perpetrator to justice. He sincerely expressed compassion, and I believed him.

Lt. Cicardo, who had just graduated from the FBI Academy in Quantico, Virginia, a short time before, was the lead questioner. I could tell he was confident and anxious to "field test" his newly acquired knowledge. The FBI Profiler Questionnaire must have been a standardized rape victim interview. The questions were detailed, intimate, and embarrassing given this "all male" company I found myself in. The men tried to be respectful, but naturally being guys, they were clueless as to how these questions would be received and interpreted by a woman victim still in the initial stages of shock. More empathetic estrogen in the room would have been a great comfort.

The exact details of the rape are hard to talk about and not appropriate for the general listening audience. The best I can do is to share a small section of a very long letter that I wrote to Hudson and Dawn on September 3, 2006—when they were grown adults, ages 25 and 23. I think the letter itself is self-explanatory, so I will quote it directly:

Sept. 3, 2006

Dear Hudson & Dawn,

... this is installment #2 in trying to fill you in on a few blanks of what happened in my life that affected you growing up and our relationship and understanding of each other now ... but no one has known all the details because I've never written down everything that happened to "us" and the emotional and mental struggles that went along with it ... Of course, the "it" I'm talking about is the attack from the serial rapist on August 19, 1987, that I survived and essentially you two "survived" also. This awful event forever changed my life and has dramatically affected me even this many years later, and even though you were young at the time, whether you realize it or not, you were traumatized too and were intrinsically a part of the rapist's profile as he secretly stalked me and you guys for the year before the actual attack...

In the aftermath of the rape, during the months of fear, anguish, and flashbacks, I received an anonymous note in the mail, written on a little piece of paper that I taped to the refrigerator, that I looked at and clung onto when I thought I just couldn't take anymore—it said, **"The will of God will not lead you where the grace of God**

cannot keep you"—*I don't understand God's ways and why things have to happen, but I have held onto the truth that "God is Sovereign"—He is always in control; nothing happens outside of His ultimate will—there is not a maverick molecule in the universe (and beyond) that is not under His control—and I can trust Him because He loves me and He does have a "good plan for my life."*

OK—here we go ... the inside, never-revealed-before facts about the rape that only I know—but affected us all—and some things that I didn't know until this past December when I was working through the fact that I was having to go through a hip replacement surgery at my "young" age that started because of the injury to my left hip over 15 years ago when the rapist taped, roped, hung me up, popped my buttock muscle, and ripped it off the bone, so it never healed right and caused osteoarthritis in that joint—I had thought I would use my six weeks of rehab time off to write a book about the unusual series of events that happened to me those few years before and after the rape and how there were some great people in the police department and in Jackson Street Presbyterian Church who helped us through it all. Alright, I hope this isn't getting too heavy for you to handle; here come some of the details of the actual attack that no one else has heard but that I want you to know—how very much I love both of you, and although

I don't consider myself any kind of a big hero—a parent's love and a mother's protection and love for her children is very strong—and that all played into the psychological profile this rapist had for his victims—strong mothers who would go through anything and do anything for the safety of their children. Here's some of what I went through mentally during that attack and during all the hard months and years afterwards.

You two slept together in the huge front bedroom—two single beds and each a green chest of drawers a nice couple from the church made for us, and all your toys—there was the living room in the front of the house as you walked in from the beautiful front porch with the swing, the bathroom, and small hallway from you guys' bedroom to mine. I had the back door and the front door locked and also deadbolted from the inside only, with a key that hung next to the light switch. I was dead tired from the weekend and went right to sleep before midnight—there were built in bookshelves right above my bed, and I always kept a long, sharpened knife there for protection, and I felt very strong and powerful because I jogged, did aerobics, and weight trained, so I could take care of myself...

I was in a complete dead sleep when someone jumped on me, and in less than 30 seconds before I was even awake or knew what was happening, he wrapped duct tape around my head, covering my eyes, threw me on the floor and roped my hands behind my back and did the same to my feet—but left a length to the rope for hanging—then I felt something cold up against my throat and heard a click and felt a switchblade come out—then I felt the blade move from my throat down to my chest and my favorite nightgown was cut off—

—all the sheets and blankets were pulled off the bed, and I was thrown back up on the bed—so much for having a weapon to protect me and being strong to defend myself—when someone has the element of surprise—none of that matters—you're never even given a chance to fight back or defend yourself—which was always hard for me to accept—the fact that I never got that chance to even try to fight my attacker.

He mumbled something about money in my purse, and I told him I didn't have any, but in the state of shock I was in, I realized that was just to make me think it was a robbery or to psyche himself up—at this point, I don't feel it's appropriate to describe in detail the hours of what went on—I've never even described it to anyone other than to answer what was necessary for the police and FBI—I'm not here to write a graphic crime novel— but ask any victim of rape—it is nothing like a romantic sexual encounter with your husband—far from it—it is all about violence and power and weapons to hurt, cause pain, and humiliate—he would grab onto the rope around my ankles and hold me upside down hanging. Of course your eyes are taped shut so you can't see what's coming next or what is going to happen or where he is or isn't—when things were quiet for a little bit, and I thought it might be over or the beginning of the "end"— he started the whole thing over again like an instant replay to get psyched again, so I got tape on top of tape and ropes on top of ropes and all the actions again— also because you can't see—only hear and feel the blade against your skin—you're never quite sure when the "end" will come and when that blade will actually go into your body and what it will feel like to be stabbed and if you can handle the pain, so you rehearse in your mind how to prepare yourself for that and to not scream and wake up your kids . . .

. . . unless your kids are already dead, and that's what you don't know during all this time—and then during the whole time to distract your mind from the reality of what is happening to you that you have no control of and no power over and you are violated, you pray all the time— and there is a sweet peace during that time and you know that you will be OK no matter what happens . . . if you live or die, and you pray for your children, Hudson and

Dawn, and you pray that the rapist spares them and that an angel protects them and that they aren't dead or suffering in the next room from something terrible he has already done to them—

—and then you pray for your enemy while he is attacking you, and you ask God to have mercy on him, and you feel sorry for him for whatever went wrong in his life that he is so sick that he has to do stuff like this to people and as you keep praying he gets less and less violent, and then there is more pain and fear, and it's hard to even concentrate on praying—and the whole time the rapist is talking to you and telling you everything about your children, your schedule, your life, and he threatens you more that he will hurt your kids (if they are still alive—you don't know), so you don't scream out loud no matter what he does to you or no matter how much it hurts because you are afraid that if Hudson and Dawn are still alive and they wake up and wander into your bedroom, then he surely will kill them at that point.

So you suffer, but you don't cry out as you are struck, and hit, and hung—and the Lord allows you to identify with His Son and to experience only a little of the pain that He endured for us when He died in our place on the cross in payment for the sins of the world and mine personally—so inside I pray and thank God that He has chosen me and He thinks I am strong enough to go through this, and I give Him glory in the midst of this suffering, and I learn how to sacrifice myself for my children because I love them more than myself.

And then there is silence.

I don't hear him in the room with me. I hear footsteps across the kitchen floor.

The back door opens and closes . . .

My message that I hope you got is that I am the same mom who went through that when you were little.

I still love you that much. It's just harder to find ways to express it now that you're grown up.

I hope there is love and healing that comes your way through this—because I do want that for you both

—Love Ya! Mom

Usually

At the conclusion of this initial interview with Captain Richie and the detectives, they did let me know that my case, which they labeled as case #4, was most probably the work of a serial rapist, and my experience fit the profile of three other cases before me ... one in December of 1985, another in the same neighborhood in February of '86, and the third across town in March '87, six months before mine. The serial rapist had stalked all of us before the attack, knew our schedules, our habits, and most likely had broken into our homes or entered before, using a hidden key he had found. None of us had dogs to alert of us an intruder, which the police said was important. A barking dog of any size would have discouraged an attacker.

After this initial interview, I had several more interviews with the officers over the next weeks to help them clarify the modus operandi of this serial guy and to exhaust every possible avenue and opportunity for a point of contact I might have had. They interviewed the Air Force buddy of my ballerina friend, Sue, who came to that Nutcracker performance and said he was "infatuated" with me. His description fit the profile, and the fact that he was military made him even more of a plausible suspect. The rapist was fastidiously clean, neat, and precise in his attacks. He left no clues, no fingerprints, no signs of entry/exit.

It was obvious that he was the obscene phone caller who first called me in December of 1986, and probably even before then, already stalking me and my children. Each of the victims were "high profile" for a small town. We had our pictures in the paper often; me with my ballet and fitness endeavors; two of the victims were doctor's wives, and the third was a banking professional and best friends with the mayor's wife. They were all socially active and involved with Junior League activities and other charitable events. Several of us taught at or were members of a local health and racquetball club. All of us were slim and attractive women. Fortunately, the officers said, the rapist left the other victims alone after the attack, so I should have no worries that he might return. Usually, a power assurance attacker will move on. Well, fortunate for the first three victims, but not so for me.

WHY ME? They don't know exactly why, but their theory was that the first three victims were married, and I was single. Perhaps the rapist developed and continued an imaginary relationship with me that he couldn't let go of. I began to get phone calls again, just weeks after the rape. Phone calls as before, but this time no conversation—just breathing from the other end of the line, but I knew it was him … he must have enjoyed that ongoing intimidation and harassment. Just another "sick" way for him to feel some sort of power over me.

They put wiretaps on my phone. The FBI limited how long they were permitted to keep them on, just ten days. The rapist would then start calling me again on day 11–how did he know? This style of rapist was categorized as a "power rapist" according to Detective Cicardo, and although the level of power and force they would use would escalate with each subsequent attack, they usually did not maim or murder … usually. I was not getting much comfort from that word.

Chapter 10

TGIFRIDAY

THURSDAY ENDED WITH me finally getting to drive over to Mr. Ayres's daughter's house. I was reunited with Hudson and Dawn and brought them back to our home; now that "the bad guy was gone, and the police were protecting us." I tried to convince myself that was true. The children already had dinner, so now we just had the bedtime routine of bath time, story time, and prayer time. I relished the superficial normality of the routine, but when it came time to say, "good night!" and close the door to go into my own bedroom, I just couldn't do it—go in there alone and sleep by myself in the same bed. I got myself ready for bed, but then I quietly snuck back into their room and crawled into bed with my sweet little Dawn. Once again, we shared her "Crunchie" blanket.

Friday was a pivotal day. My dad and Mamoo were still staying at the motel. My children had to switch custody, and I had to get them ready to go stay for the weekend with their dad. Also, I had a 4:00 p.m. pre-scheduled session down in Baton Rouge, about a two-and-a-half-hour drive, with my psychologist, Dr. Donald Hoppe, to continue working on my recovery from anorexia and related self-image issues. I was thankful for the good fortune of already having had this appointment set up … I really needed to talk to a professional counselor.

I had choices to make, and I made them based on what everybody else needed from me, not what I wanted or needed. Mamoo's birthday was the next day, August 22. I knew what I had to do. I woke up the kids Friday morning and told them, "Guess what? Mamoo and Poppa came to visit us for Mamoo's big birthday celebration, and they are staying at the motel close by waiting for us. We are going to get dressed up nice for her and then go to the grocery store to pick out a card and cake with birthday candles to surprise her!"

Children are so wonderfully innocent and naïve … they didn't question the timing or the logic of it all. They just enthusiastically got dressed to go see their "Poppa" and get birthday goodies for their great grandmother. Before we left the house, I called my dad at the motel to tell him of our plans and impending visit … he was understandably touched. It was ironic that here I was in the middle of my big meltdown, but I had to reach out and be sure that Mamoo and my family were OK about MY tragedy! This was exactly why I didn't want them to come.

"Welcome to Greenville, The Blackest Land, The Whitest People"[16]

This part of my story, exposing the prejudice of my southern born and bred grandmother, makes me sad to even relay. Only by God's **grace** to me and the counterbalancing influence of my other grandmother, "Mom-Mom," my mother's mother, did I not harbor any of the racial prejudices that surrounded me growing up. The East Texas town, Greenville, where my parents grew up and married had a "welcome sign" for visitors declaring, "Welcome to Greenville, The Blackest Land, The Whitest People."

It is shocking to us, in our modern time of ethnic diversity and acceptance, that such a sign could have even existed and was not even removed until the 1960s. Mamoo had told me that it meant all the people there were "pure" and "white" in heart. I didn't buy into that line of reasoning, and where Mamoo truly stood on the subject was exposed when she learned that I had invited a "Black girl" to the high school senior luncheon she was throwing for me at the exclusive Petroleum Club in Dallas.

Debbie was a good friend and a popular school cheerleader, so it never occurred to me that I should mention that she was also Black. Mamoo was horrified when she found out just days before the event. What if "somebody" might see a Negro girl eating with White folk at our table and tell some of her friends in Greenville! My grandmother threatened to not give me my graduation gift, a diamond ring, if I didn't uninvite Debbie. Not happening! Mom-Mom, my genuinely Christian grandmother, was seated next to Debbie at the far end of the table from Mamoo, and we all had a wonderful time. Unfortunately for Mamoo, there happened to be another table of girls next to us who were also there for their senior luncheon—yes, from Greenville, Texas—so I guess word got out anyway.

Hudson and Dawn were genuinely excited to go to the motel and see their Poppa and Mamoo ... my family has always been generous, supportive, and very loving towards my kids. But while the children were occupied wrestling and having fun with Poppa, Mamoo found time to speak with me privately to inform me that she had read the morning *Town Talk* newspaper, which elaborated on my case and revealed an important fact ... important to her anyway. Evidently, the rapist was less aggressive and violent in his earlier attacks, and he tried to use panty hose to secure his victim's wrists and to cover their eyes. One of the earlier victims was able to free her hands and pull off the blindfold and get a glimpse of her attacker ... so that she could identify him as a "White male with blondish hair, with a slim build."

"Well," my grandmother concluded, "what a relief that you weren't raped by a Black man. Now you should just go on and forget this incident ever happened ... don't tell anybody about it and get on with your life and taking care of your children." According to her it will be gone with the wind! I remember trying to stand up to her and telling her, "How dare you say or think that! My eyes were taped shut in the first 30 seconds of the attack—it didn't matter if I was raped by a purple, green, Black, or White man ... nothing could have made that better by what skin color he had—can't you understand that?" Sadly, she couldn't. She was a prisoner of her time. In her eyes, everything was absolved because the rapist was White—not Black.

I think they ordered in pizza for an early lunch to be delivered at the motel—I was delighted that my kids were enjoying the visit and were happy but then it was time to take them to the YWCA for the custody switch. Ms. Masden made sure that they were in very caring hands for the afternoon, so I was free to leave early and drive to Baton Rouge for my late afternoon appointment. How I ever kept going and did the next thing, and the next thing, I have no idea … I am just NOT that courageous, no matter what I would like to think. It was only by an extraordinary gift of strength that enabled me to move forward … it was a "God Thing" as we would say now … it was a **"Re- and Me"** adventure. Again, God's grace!

Dr. Hoppe validated all that I felt as I went through this horrendous experience. He reassured me that we would continue moving forward in my therapy and healing. I had been coming to Dr. Hoppe off and on since my brother's suicide in 1983 (paid for secretly by my Christian grandmother, Mom-Mom, since Mamoo didn't "believe" in psychology). I left his office with hope that—with continued therapy and help from my friends at church and the YWCA—I might get through this. I gassed up the car, got my traditional peanut butter crackers to eat on the way home, and started back to Alexandria. All was good until I entered the southern city limits of Alexandria as the sun was beginning to set … darkness would come soon, and I would have to go to my house—the scene of the crime—ALONE—no children to pretend to be brave for—just me, alone.

I panicked—finally, I let myself be a human being who is also a woman and feel the full impact of the past few days. I knew I absolutely could NOT go home alone! Who did I know around here? Where was I? Oh, I recognize those railroad tracks, this subdivision — my aerobics friend, JoAnne Soileau, also from our church, lives close by. I have been to her house before and met her husband and girls. Could I find it again? I wandered up and down streets with an increasing panic as the sun sunk lower, until I recognized their home. It was even darker now. I parked the car in their driveway and literally ran up to their door and pounded on it—I felt like something vampirish was going to happen to me if the sun set and I was left in darkness. Her husband, Paul, came to the door and stepped out onto their front porch. I didn't have to explain; I knew that everyone in our church had been in on a "prayer chain" of phone calls and knew all about what had happened to me. I literally fell into his arms and started blubbering about how scared I was and how I couldn't go back home by myself and where was JoAnne and when would she be back home?

Her husband, Paul, did the most incredible thing … he gave me that big bear hug thing and let me collapse in his arms and cry. Then finally, he let loose slightly and brought me into the entryway of their home—away from the eyes of neighbors who might misinterpret what they saw. I was like a ragdoll in his arms as I sobbed and wailed.

This was the first time since the rape that I was able to quit pretending to be so brave and strong for everyone else and cry openly and unashamedly. He kept patting me on the head and on my shoulders, like I was his little daughter who was hurting and kept whispering to me, "It's OK, don't worry. It will be OK. God is good. Not all men are bad. God is going to give you a good man someday." He kept repeating versions of that over and over as he comforted me. I don't know how long I stood there like a weeping child in his arms, but eventually, I was able to walk into his den and he seated me on a stool at his bar.

I was never a drinker, maybe some wine or cocktails on special occasions, but I had never had a taste of hard liquor. He poured me a drink of something strong and said to consider it medicine to help calm me down. I was on my second glass of "medicine" when JoAnne arrived home from her grocery shopping. They both let me know that I was safe with them, and I could stay all weekend. I could sleep in their daughter's bedroom … she was at a slumber party with girlfriends. Amazing **Grace!** How could God have guided me directly to this special couple who were able give me exactly the kind of emotional help I needed at this moment?

That night, I had a severe episode of post-traumatic stress. I would wake up often during the night, with flashbacks, screaming uncontrollably. It was always Paul, not JoAnne, who would come into the room to compassionately hug me and offer me father-like words of comfort. It was immensely healing for me to have a "big brother friend"—a strong male whom I could trust and wouldn't hurt me—to reassure me during the night. As the days unfolded, the men who were most helpful, most compassionate, empathetic and understanding were the police captain and detectives on the scene who knew what victims like me had gone through, the mature leaders in my church: Pastor Bob Vincent, Dick Ayres, Paul Soileau, and some other caring men and husbands from our congregation.

I woke up late Saturday morning, not in the best physical condition—but what did I expect from the culmination of the events from the past four days? Over a cup of coffee, I talked over with the Soileau's what I could do to try and get some sense of control and power over my life. One thing I remembered from the police profiling was that none of the victims had a dog, big or little. A barking dog seemed to deter criminal endeavors. So, if I had the choice, it seemed to me that BIG was better! I looked in the local newspaper and found an ad for German Shepard puppies for sale. After several phone calls, I was put in touch with a breeder who specifically bred large bone German Shepherds for police training. I let them know that I wasn't interested in a cute little puppy … I needed a BIG ready-to-bite attack dog! They had the perfect dog for me, a six-month old female. They said she was young enough to still be trained, but already big enough at 60 pounds to provide protection. The breeders said they expected her to be a 90 pounds tour de force, fully grown.

I literally had less than $200 in my personal account, but I took my checkbook and drove out to the countryside location where the dogs were kenneled. The establishment was run by retired law enforcement officers, and I'm sure that I got a discounted price when they heard my story and why I needed a large dog … I purchased a huge bag of dog food, a collar, a training leash, and signed papers to purchase my protector whom I named "Hilarry"—the middle name of my daughter. "Hilarry," with its variation on the traditional spelling was in honor of my dear brother, Larry, who passed away from a suicide three weeks before my daughter's birth. Hillary means "Cheerful-Joyful-Hilarious!" which fit my daughter perfectly, and she was named after Sir Edmond Hillary, who in the year of my birth, 1953 along with his Nepalese Sherpa, Tenzin, were the first climbers to ever reach the summit of Mount Everest. Courage, perseverance, and fortitude … those were qualities I admired and attributes I needed to acquire if I was to ever get through this latest character challenge.

Hilarry was huge! Her head alone was twice the size of my daughter's face, and her giant clumsy feet revealed that she had room to grow. It was empowering to have her seated beside me in the car driving back to the Soileau's house, with her big happy head hanging out the window. It was worth it, even if we both had to eat dog food for the next month! Her intimidating presence made me feel strong again. Surely, no one would think about messing with me with this humongous dog by my side. I was able to go back to the Soileau's home Saturday afternoon with Hilarry in tow, say thank you and then return to my own home. I took her for a walk around my neighborhood Saturday afternoon (or rather she took me for a walk!), and I felt secure. I slept alone in my home that night with Hilarry snuggled next to me, albeit in Dawn's bed, not yet in my own bed ... but it was progress in overcoming my fears!

Sunday, I had an uneventful day—with my big girl, Hilarry—walking together, getting to know each other. I was intent on recuperating and getting to a calmer place. I was able to get the children Sunday evening from weekend custody with their dad—and introduce them to our protector, Hilarry. It was love at first lick!!

Chapter 11

THE QUESTION

AFTER THE INITIAL SHOCK of the rapist attack had subsided, and I was attempting to get back into some sort of routine, rhythm, and sense of normalcy, I had to confront some difficult questions. Some of those questions were just thrown in my face ... I didn't see them coming, and they hit me hard.

With all the mystery that surrounds you as the *special victim* of a sexually based crime, it was terrifying to go out into public again. Unfortunately, since my profession was to get up in front of people and teach dance and fitness, I didn't have the luxury of hiding out for very long. To protect the privacy of the victims, the media were not allowed to give out names in the newspaper or TV, so I was always referred to as the "Woman in the Garden District." Yet, for years it has bothered me that victims of rape were treated differently ...

people would become uncomfortable in the course of a regular conversation with me when in passing I mentioned that I was a victim of a serial **RAPIST**, or that such and such happened after the **r- - -**. It was a four-letter word that I wasn't supposed to use in polite conversation. I never got that. If I had said, "After I was robbed at knifepoint," or "after I was shot during a bank heist," no one would have been as shocked if I was just an innocent victim of a criminal who used a knife or a gun as his weapon of choice, but that logic doesn't transfer over when the crime is **rape,** and the criminal uses his sex organ as his weapon. Suddenly my integrity came into question.

In a small southern town, people talk … either in front of you to others or behind your back, or to themselves—judging you in their own minds. Criticism can come to you from the least likely and unexpected people—those who you thought would have your back, and sometimes from those who call themselves "Christian." It was the first Sunday after the attack that the children were not with their dad for weekend custody, and we could go to Sunday school and worship service together. In the past, if the children had been cooperative in getting dressed and ready for church on time, their reward was to go to Shipley's Donuts and pick out their favorite treat for breakfast.

This time, I was the one who had trouble getting myself dressed to go out in public to see and be seen by some people for the first time after the assault. I had an anxiety attack, and if it had not been to please Hudson and Dawn, who were excited to see their friends at church, I could have easily stayed home. There was no drive-up window back then, so we went inside to pick out our donuts. On my way out, as I was walking towards the door, my ophthalmologist, who used to be a leader in our church, left his table and came across to speak to me. I was expecting my doctor to express his condolences to say he was sorry about what happened to me—or to say that he was or would be praying for me and the children, but I could NEVER have been prepared for what he DID say to me:

"I heard what happened to you and I'm sorry ... I'm sorry that I didn't come to you sooner—before—because I just knew this would happen to you because of what you do ... wearing exercise clothes getting up in front of people and your picture in the paper. I should have warned you."

I was so shocked, I couldn't even respond verbally—I must have mumbled a "thanks" as I left and then I struggled to hold back the tears as I buckled kids in car seats, drove to church, and signed them into their Sunday school classes. Then, I had to go back out to the car in the parking lot where I could sob and cry without anyone seeing me. What was THAT all about? Was my doctor saying what I thought he was saying, or was he just the first one who got into my face and virtually asked "The Question" that everyone else was thinking?

The QUESTION IS: DID I "ASK FOR IT?"

... Because I'm female and God naturally made my body proportionate and attractive to men?

... Because I exercise and have a fit body?

... Because I go out jogging on the streets in shorts?

... Because I sunbathe in my backyard?

... Because I'm in the dance and fitness business?

I was still upset on the following Monday morning when I went back to work teaching a few private sessions at the YWCA. I remember telling Ms. Masden what my ophthalmologist had said to me, and I asked her if she thinks I deserved getting raped ... if I somehow "asked for it." I'll never forget the answer my conservative Catholic boss gave me:

> "No woman 'asks to be raped.' No man has the right to use his power over you to touch you sexually in any way against your will or unspoken desire, without your permission—whether you are conscious or unconscious, especially if you are unconscious! I don't care if you sunbathe in your bikini in the backyard or prance around naked in your front yard—that doesn't give anyone the right to sexually touch or assault you!!"

The Question

I especially remembered the "prance around your yard naked" part—she had me laughing at that. Her voice was so passionate and strong that I felt the certainty of her convictions. This was 1987. She was decades ahead of the "#MeToo" movement.

Tuesday afternoon I was in the kitchen when the doorbell rang, and of course, I was nervous going to the door. I looked out the window first and saw a woman, so I cautiously opened a crack in the door. Right away I recognized the by now familiar badge ... Child Protection Services! Are you kidding me?! She handed me the papers and told me what I was accused of:

"Bringing a strange man into my home overnight and endangering my children."

Talk about "kicking the proverbial dog while he's down"! Imagine how incensed I was, having just survived the overnight attack by the rapist, who threatened to harm my children while I suffered and kept from screaming to protect my children. And now, you insult me by saying that I "brought a strange man into my home"?

Whoever filed this anonymous false child abuse report is a totally disgusting person! I took the papers and tried hard not be rude and angry at the messenger—she was only doing her job, and I knew enough to realize that there really are situations out there where the children do need protection. But make no mistake—I was extremely angry. I was furious at the anonymous tipster using Child Protection Services as an agent of harassment to target me, but who instead was harming my children. Knowing all that they went through with me after the attack, I was one who was most concerned about their emotional well-being. And now, because of this latest false child abuse accusation (I was up to seven at this point and still counting!), they were going to have to be taken off into a room away from me to go through another "interview." They would be asked questions like, "Does your mommy bring over strange men to your house who scare you?" and other such garbage that would plant seeds of fear and doubt when I was doing everything I possibly could to minimize their insecurities and trauma.

I turned to my own ferocious "attack dog"—none other than Ms. Masden. She would know how to fight this unjust system. Indeed, Ms. Ann went directly to the district attorney on my and the children's behalf. She came back with a whole lot of information about the state laws concerning child protection and a half-win in that the DA waived the children having to endure another interview and surprise observation visit.

But me? No special favors for recent rape victims.

I got to go through yet another full investigation and questioning by the agency. The anonymous tipsters can file as many complaints as they want, and the CPS, by law, must investigate each one. If a complaint is filed, such as not feeding the children properly, and the defendant's case was investigated and closed, then the tipsters can't use that particular complaint for a set window of time.

The Question

They have to creatively come up with another type of false accusation. And, it helps to have a conspiracy of false accusers—different associates who can call in different accusations to make it more convincing to CPS. It is an endless merry-go-round that robs precious resources of time and money from the overloaded agency who needs to investigate true abuse cases. Although none of the final reports of the investigations are allowed in the courts during child custody litigation, that doesn't stop the vindictive divorcee from using the process to harass his ex-partner and mentioning in court that there were investigations by CPS. There were over 12 false cases filed against me and investigated before I left the state of Louisiana…

DID I "ASK FOR IT?"

Chapter 12

ALL MEN ARE JERKS!

All men are JERKS!

My ex is a JERK.

His guy fellow workers at CenLa Ambulance are blind following the blind JERKS.

His guy friends who anonymously filed countless false child abuse reports are stupid JERKS.

His good ole boy lawyer is a JERK with no scruples.

The officials who authorized my arrest for threatening murder with no evidence are idiotic JERKS.

The doctor in the ER at the Rape Crises Center is an insensitive JERK.

The doctors at my OB/GYN office are sort of misled JERKS.

My ophthalmologist who said, "He knew this would happen to me because I teach aerobics" is an ignorant JERK.

And the serial rapist is the **Ultimate Cowardly Despicable JERK!**

I have a logical dilemma with my premise: ALL men are JERKS! Jesus came to earth as a man (how convenient for Him!)

Is Jesus a JERK too?

This logical dilemma became a major spiritual battle and personal crises for me in the weeks after the rape. Jesus was my best friend who had saved me and rescued me.

"Jesus loves me, this I know, for the Bible tells me so."

All Men Are Jerks!

But wait! Jesus is a male. He was incarnate as a man.

How can Jesus possibly identify with me, a WOMAN who has just been violently raped by a man and treated unfairly by other men?

How can Jesus possibly understand what I'm going through as a FEMALE who was sexually assaulted? And oh, by the way ... I really can't talk to your dad about it either.

"Our Father who art in heaven" (Matthew 6:9).

God is a guy too. I'm stuck.

What would Jesus possibly know about being surprised in the middle of the night and made a prisoner?

What would He know about being blindfolded with your eyes covered, so you couldn't even see who it was who was attacking or striking you?

How could He even understand the humiliation of being stripped, with your nakedness uncovered?

How could He feel what it was like to have ropes bound tightly around your wrists, cutting off your circulation, or your feet crossed and wrapped securely, so you couldn't move them?

Does He know what it's like to feel dehumanized—to have your body controlled and abused by someone else? Has He had something stuck in and wrapped around your head, pulling out your hair?

Have His muscles been stretched to the point of tearing, with your joints pulled out of place? Would He have any idea what it's like to be mocked and ridiculed verbally by an attacker?

Has He had to force Himself to keep silent as a lamb and not cry out, even during the most excruciating pain? Has He felt the sharp metal blade against His skin waiting to pierce Him??

"Pierced? Silent as a lamb"? Wait, I've read this all somewhere before:

> *"Surely our griefs He Himself bore, and our sorrows He carried;*

Yet we ourselves esteemed Him stricken, smitten of God, and afflicted.

But He was pierced through for our transgressions, He was crushed for our iniquities; The chastening for our well-being fell upon Him, and by His scourging we are healed. All of us like sheep have gone astray, each of us has turned to his own way;

But the LORD has caused the iniquity of us all to fall on Him.

He was oppressed and He was afflicted, yet He did not open His mouth;

Like a lamb that is led to slaughter, and like a sheep that is silent before its shearers,

So He did not open His mouth"

(Isaiah 53: 4-7).

This Old Testament prophecy was written around 700-740 B.C. (Before Christ) but describes His crucifixion.

Re- *and* Me

Maybe, just maybe He does understand.

Maybe He can identify with me.

Maybe it's possible that He does know what I've been through.

Could it be that He knows because He suffered and went through all that for humankind?

My heart had become so calloused in my anger towards MEN in general, and Jesus by way of association, that when I realized the truth about my Jesus, I emotionally broke down in that rare moment of connection.

He came to earth as a vulnerable human male, suffering for mankind and womankind.

"For we do not have a high priest who cannot sympathize with our weaknesses, but One who has been tempted in all things as we are, yet without sin. Therefore let us draw near with confidence to the throne of grace, so that we may receive mercy and find grace to help in time of need"

(Hebrews 4: 15-16).

Re- my little friend—**GRACE**—find me, **re**mind me who Jesus is and how He **re**deemed me.

All Men Are Jerks!

Jesus, in His passion to **re**deem me, suffered and identified with me in every way:

He was captured and arrested in the middle of the night by the Jewish leaders and their soldiers. After His unjust trial, He was turned over to the Roman soldiers where He was blindfolded, mocked, struck with rods and scourged.

He had a crown of sharp thorns wrapped around His head, pressed into His scalp.

His robes were stripped off, and His nakedness was exposed—save a cloth around His loins. He was led to Golgotha, prompted by the blade of a Roman spear.

His hands and feet were tied then nailed to the cross.

He hung in excruciating pain as the weight of His body pulled His joints out of place.

He kept silent and didn't retaliate or cry out against His accusers and abusers.

His side was pierced by a Roman soldier so that blood and water flowed to confirm His death.

I get it now! He understands. JESUS "GETS" ME!!!

Re- *and* Me

NO! My Jesus isn't a JERK...

He is kind, caring, compassionate, and **re**spectful to women.

And any men who identify with Jesus in their attitudes and actions are the same ... I can trust them.

Yes, some men are JERKS...

But NOT ALL men are jerks.

Chapter 13

THE STRANGEST REQUEST

I CONTINUED TO STRUGGLE in the days that followed with the guilt and shame of having been a rape victim. Because of the ongoing custody battle and all the false child abuse reports, I could not let any chinks in my armor show. I was able to get my children into counseling and "play therapy" for child witnesses of violent crimes, but I could not risk being seen going to counseling myself. My ex and his lawyer might use that against me to say that I was too unstable to parent the children and then file another motion for change of custody.

I reached a crisis point as I continued to struggle with that first **QUESTION:** "Did I ask for it?"

But the second **QUESTION** that would haunt me was even more insidious:

"If my hands and feet weren't tied and taped right away, would I have fought him, or did I really 'want it'?"

Isn't this what most men believe ... that secretly I really wanted sex with them?

Because I was rendered "passive" during the attack, the guilt and shame were intensified:

1. I'm guilty of allowing this to happen or somehow not responding soon enough in those first surprising 30 seconds coming out of a dead sleep and fighting him off to the death.
2. I'm ashamed because I wasn't strong enough physically to overcome his male strength and cunning—I didn't master self-defense techniques.
3. I'm guilty of being born a woman—the weaker sex—I'm not equal; I'm vulnerable. I have less muscle mass than males—I'm at a disadvantage—it's unfair.

Finally, I felt like I just couldn't go on anymore, and I went to Pastor Bob at my cracking point. I distinctly remember our whole conversation standing outside his office. I appreciate his wisdom in talking with me as we stood in the hallway—an earshot from the secretary's open door so that there was no question of impropriety but private enough for me to blurt out my worst thoughts about myself:

The Strangest Request

I told him, "I can't go on anymore—everyone knows who I am—I'm 'The Woman in the Garden District.' I'm the local aerobic queen, and I deserved this because I wear leotards and tights just like Dr. XXX said! I didn't fight the rapist off hard enough to stop it, so I must have wanted it. It is all my fault. I should have been more careful, less attractive, had more muscle mass, less media attention!!"

Pastor Bob assured me, "That is a lie! That is a cruel lie directly out of the pit of hell! What do you believe? What do you really think about yourself? Do you think you would have fought him if you could, if you had the chance?"

Here is where somehow my darkest fears came jumping out of the shadows, frightening me into blurting out words that I didn't want to own.

"I don't know—I don't know! I think I would have. I hope I would have. I want to think so. I always thought I was a fighter, but now I don't know! How could I let this happen? How do I know what I would have done when I never even got the chance? I'm angry! I'm angry I never got a shot. I'm so angry about that—but I can't get angry at the rapist. I never saw him; it was dark, and my eyes were taped shut—to me he is faceless—nameless. Only

I listen for his voice everywhere I go—wondering if this guy or that clerk is him."

Pastor Bob lowered his voice decibels below mine and said quietly, "Sandy is angry at the rapist. My wife is angry at what he has done to you and the other women."

"I know." I said. "That's the whole point—all the women around me in my life are ticked off. Ann Masden and Denise Van Bibber at the YW are furious at the chauvinistic male attitude around town.

So far, all four of us—his rape victims—were youngish, fit, attractive—and the macho male consensus seem to think it was our fault. According to the *Town Talk* newspaper, the rapist is a 'gentleman'—that is what they've dubbed him all across the front pages, '*The Gentleman Rapist*'![17] It is insulting to any woman. Excuse me! The rapist is now a "gentleman" because he carried one of the victims from the bed to the bathroom so she could use the toilet and then carried her back to the bed so he could finish raping her? Oh, how very thoughtful of him!! Are you kidding me? I'm angry at the *Town Talk* publishing that and the jerk guy editor that signed off on that, but I just can't get into getting angry at the rapist. I don't personally feel angry at him."

Pastor Bob asked me the question that had to be asked. "Then what do you feel? What do you feel about the rapist?"

"I don't feel anything," I first said, but when those words came out, I knew they weren't true. "I think what I feel, what I mostly feel is sadness. I feel sorry for him. I feel sad that he is such a pathetic little person that he needs to make himself feel powerful and important by using his male sex organ to dominate women—demeaning them. What went wrong with him? What made him such a Sicko?

What happened to him?"

The pastor was incredulous. "What happened to HIM?" he questioned. "What happened to HIM?" he said again, raising his voice. "What about what happened to YOU?! Look what he's done to YOU, to YOUR life. Aren't you angry about that? Look at how he's tried to destroy you—to undo you. What about Hudson and Dawn—your children? Look what happened to them ... how he's harmed them emotionally and the memories they will have to carry with them—surely you are angry about that!"

"I know, I am so protective and angry for them," I admitted to the pastor through my tears that were now starting to flow, "for what he took away from us—from them—our security—our peace of mind—their innocence. But for myself, I just can't 'GO' there."

"What do you mean by that?" Pastor Bob pressed me.

"I mean I'm afraid of what would happen if I really allowed the feelings to come out," I clarified for him and myself. "If I got into my anger … I don't know … I might lose it. I might totally crack up and fall apart and never make it back. I heard that one of the victims before me had to go into a mental hospital."

Pastor Bob said, "But losing it could be good. Do you see that it could be good? Your anger is there deep inside somewhere. Finding and facing your anger could be part of your healing. Can you see that? I have a strange request for you. I want you to slap me hard on my cheek right here," he said as he pointed to the side of his face.

"What?!!" I protested, "I can't do that! You're the pastor. I can't hit you!" "I'm telling you it's OK," he said, "I want you to slap me."

"Are you nuts? Seriously?" I said as I half-heartedly slapped his face with the palm of my hand.

The Strangest Request

"I don't believe that. Slap me hard—really hard," the pastor commanded me.

"I'll try to do better," I said as I heard a smack this time when I slapped him.

"That's good. Do it again. And now again. And the other cheek too. Go ahead—hit me—hit him again," he instructed me. "If your hands were free would you fight him? Would you hit him? Would you protect yourself—would you protect your children? What about Hudson and Dawn? You would fight to protect them ... HIT HIM AGAIN! Slap me again," he insisted.

By this time, I was shaking, slapping, and crying all at the same time. My own defenses were breaking down and I lost awareness of where I was as I sobbed and slapped. This last time, Pastor Bob reached up to catch my wrist to stop me, and I shook off his hold on my wrist and slapped him anyway.

Then he said, "OK, that's good—that's enough," as he put his arm across my shoulder for a moment and gave me a father-like pat. "God's hands aren't tied," he told me, "God is able to do anything—nothing is impossible with God. Right now, what is one impossible thing that you don't think God can do?"

"I don't know," I sobbed, "but a crazy thought just popped into my head."

"Nothing is too crazy for God," he assured me. "That's it; what is the impossible crazy thing you want to ask God to do?"

I shared with him my crazy thought, telling him, "Right now, I can't imagine my younger brother coming to the Lord—becoming a Christian. I lost my older brother to suicide. Only God knows the state of his soul at the moment of his death. I want to believe that God can reach down and get ahold of my younger brother's heart. It seems impossible."

Bob said, "Let's believe God for this seemingly impossible prayer request for true salvation for your younger brother and for you to get angry and break free from your guilt."

Pastor Bob enclosed his hands in a protective way around my hands as he prayed for me. I don't remember his exact words, and some words were in another language—maybe even a heavenly language—I don't know because I was sniffling loudly, and tears were pouring down my own cheeks, but he prayed with confidence, acknowledging that all power to accomplish anything comes from God. He prayed for me—that I would find healing and victory over my shame and guilt—that I would find the anger I have pressed down and be released from it. He prayed for protection for me, and for God to remove all fears from my children. He prayed for my "impossible thing," that in His own time that He would bring my younger brother to a saving faith in the Lord Jesus. He closed the prayer by affirming that "God is able to do exceedingly abundantly beyond all that we ask or think. (Ephesians 3:20)—in the powerful name of Jesus, Amen."

It was a little awkward as I opened my eyes from the prayer and noticed that his face had red marks from where I had slapped him. "I am sorry if I hurt you," I told him. "That was weird—why did you have me do that?"

My pastor replied, "I don't know—it's what God gave me. I quit asking Him 'why' a long time ago. He doesn't have to explain Himself to me. My job is to listen to the Spirit as He speaks to me and obey."

Then he added, "These verses came to me:

'BE ANGRY, AND *yet* DO NOT SIN; do not let the sun go down on your anger ...' (Ephesians 4:26).

'For you, being *so* wise, tolerate the foolish gladly. For you tolerate it if anyone enslaves you, anyone devours you, anyone takes advantage of you, anyone exalts himself, anyone hits you in the face' (2 Corinthians 11:19-20).

"Before you can 'not let the sun go down on your anger' and find forgiveness for your attacker, you first need to 'be angry'. Be righteously angry and **re**fuse to tolerate what has happened to you," advised Pastor Bob.

I thanked the pastor for his wisdom and told him that I did feel again. I felt anger. I waited for healing.

The Dream

The next several weeks, Pastor Bob preached through a series of sermons on the subject, "Dreams and Visions," expounding on the idea that if God spoke directly to His prophets and people in biblical days through visions, He is still able to use dreams today. He said it was his personal conviction that sometimes the Lord used our seemingly random dreams to speak to us and **re**veal a personal message.

I didn't have to worry about dreams because I didn't have any. The first week after the attack, I couldn't sleep at all, and if I did fall asleep for a bit, I would wake up with flashbacks and nightmares. I would put the children down to bed after their bedtime stories and prayers, then I would walk through the hall to try and open the door of my bedroom, but a panic attack would greet me at the door each night, and I had to **re**treat and go back and lay down with one of the kids in their bed, with Hilarry on the floor beside us. I just couldn't go back into my own bed at night—the fear was immense. Finally, I was so exhausted that I went back to my OB/GYN, and he gave me a limited prescription for AMBIEN, a strong sleeping pill. Most of the supportive women around me had another one of those "guys don't get it moments!" and couldn't believe that my male OB/GYN hadn't already prescribed them for a rape victim. Well, those pills provided sweet **re**lief from my terrors, and I would fall asleep almost immediately after I took them and stay asleep the whole night until my alarm went off in the morning.

The only time this pattern was broken was a few weeks after Pastor Bob began to preach about the significance of dreams and how God could use them to speak to us. This night I woke up about 4:00 a.m.—hours before daylight—with my heart pounding and my body in an elevated state of fight or flight. My mind was alert, all five senses were engaged at a heightened level … I was there again. It was the night of the rape, and the rapist was on top of me, but this time I wasn't helpless. My hands were wrestled free from the ropes and duct tape, so I was able to fight off my attacker. I slapped him and punched him hard in the face with my fists and then of all things, I grabbed his head—twisted it to the side and bit off his ear! He fled.

Right then I woke up from the dream with the very real taste of blood in my mouth. I was shocked that I could be capable of such anger and violence myself. It was "just a dream"—how could I control a dream or be **re**sponsible for what I visualized? I was shaken, and at sunrise, since it was Saturday and I knew they were early risers, I called Sandy Vincent and asked if I could come over and bring the kids—I had a scary but significant dream I wanted to share with her and Bob.

Their older teenage children played with my kids while I spoke with the Bob and Sandy over coffee (drinking coffee together is a huge Cajun custom). I related the details of my dream and what a terrible savage thing I did by biting off the rapist's ear. (footnote: I must have originated the idea—this was 1987, and Mike Tyson the boxer didn't have his infamous ear biting episode until 1997)[18]. What a horrible person I must be to angrily beat and bite him, but instead of being shocked, they were smiling at each other and telling me, "Praise the Lord!"

"Praise the Lord? Praise the Lord! That's what you have to say? How could you possibly be happy about it? What I dreamt is awful—I must be as bad a person as he is," I said, hiding behind my guilt and shame. This was not the **re**sponse I was expecting to get.

"Don't you see?" Bob said. "This is the answer to our prayer to free you from your guilt. God gave you your answer in loud, living color—sight and sound! **Re**member—your haunting question when you came to me for counsel was that if your hands had been free during the attack, would you have fought him off to protect yourself and your children? The answer is YES! You ARE a fighter—you didn't want this, and you didn't ask for it!"

He went on, "Your answer from God is a big 'bloody' YES! You can now be set free from your doubts. You don't have to carry that guilt and shame anymore. God has given you the breakthrough we asked Him for, and you can move forward into that place of peace and forgiveness. Let's pray together now to thank Him and pray again for your brother, that he will get his breakthrough too."

Chapter 14

THE KEY

THE RAPIST CONTINUED his silent campaign of intimidation and continued to "check in" on me with his heavy breathing phone calls in between wiretaps. I had already determined that he wasn't going to win this fight. "Success is the Best Revenge" became my motto, and success was now defined as simply living, working, caring for my children, and NOT falling apart. I was going to show him that he picked the wrong woman to mess with. I wasn't going to break, no matter what! Well, his "what" did mess with my mind and brought me close to the brink.

By the first of October, I was back to teaching all my classes at the YWCA, the Pre-School Creative Movement programs in the daycare centers, and my weekend F.U.N. Fitness Certification Seminars ... the next one was scheduled for mid-October. I had sent out a large mail out of brochures along with copies of the news article of Joyce Ward's visit, ran my ads in the *Town Talk* newspaper, and rented out the LSU-Alexandria site. I was ready, and thankfully the registrations rolled in so that I was close to capacity. Having had the experience of conducting multiple seminars by now—I had the Friday "prep" routine down. I loaded up the fitness mats and stereo system I borrowed from the YW after I finished my morning classes and then dropped by the house to load up all the aerobic notebooks and tapes. For some reason I decided to check my mailbox and grab the mail to read while I was at the hair salon.

I wore the famous frizzy perm style of the 80s; think *Dirty Dancing*—1987 with Jennifer Grey and Patrick Swayze. Unfortunately, that hairstyle didn't hold up too well for a two-day full-out aerobic sweat fest. I discovered that getting a professional stylist to "French braid" my hair with gel and spray, along with the mandatory headband, kept it in place throughout the weekend. I sat in the salon chair trying to calm my mind for the intense amount of focus it would take to lead a large group through the learning process of a certification. I shuffled through the stack of mail that had accumulated in my mailbox over the past few days. Hmmm ... there was an envelope addressed to me personally but with no return address—postmarked San Antonio. I don't know a single person from there. While my hairdresser chatted away, I opened the envelope and pulled out a blank card. There, taped to the card was my deadbolt key!!! In an automatic response, my fingers opened suddenly, and I dropped the card in my lap, letting out a gasp as if I had just picked up a poisonous snake.

My stylist also jumped back and screamed, "What is it? What is it? What's wrong?" I directed her to bring me a clean towel to wrap up the envelope, card, and key and then asked to use the phone. I was shaking all over, and my voice quivered as I asked the operator for the police department—detective division. I was way past trying to be discreet with the other patrons in the salon, and in a loud frantic voice I told the detective who I was, where I was, and that I needed them to come immediately to pick up this piece of evidence in my case. And, I really wanted to say, "I told you so!" I knew I had heard the rapist go out the back door even though both doors were locked with the deadbolt and the keys were still on the hook.

Lt. Cicardo confirmed that it was the key to my deadbolt. The only explanation was that the rapist, who knew my schedule, broke into my home through the loose window before the attack on a night I was teaching late, stole the deadbolt key off the hook, left and got a copy made for himself, and then returned my original key to the hook, so I wouldn't notice. He then used his copy to let himself into my home on Tuesday night, and there were signs that he hid in the back of my bedroom closet waiting for me to fall asleep. How creepy! How disturbing! How NUTS was it for the rapist to mail back my key on this very day—this Friday of my first seminar back after the attack. It's true! He was still following me through my newspaper ads, by telephone, and maybe even stalking me again. How did I know he wouldn't be at the seminar waiting for me after I finish … to finish me off?

Lt. Cicardo understood my fears, even though he thought this serial rapist was too much of a coward to be a killer. However, the rapist had escalated his level of violence with each subsequent attack, changed the profile of his target victim in my case from married to single, and unlike the other three women before me, he continued to harass me after the attack. He was evolving. It was a cat and mouse game between him and the detectives—mailing the key back to me was a taunt. Deviant sexual behavior and psychological profiling became an obsession often on Lt. Thomas Circado's mind, according to the book he published in 2005, *Because They Can*. Thomas "had been going over old case files and comparing notes from classes at the FBI Academy. He started thinking of how he could apply all this knowledge from Quantico to these cases."[19]

The detectives agreed that they would send an unmarked police car and officers to watch the building and escort me home after the seminar Friday and Saturday night. My mother, Beth, always said I was a "born performer" and that ability to turn off the world and turn it on when it was "show time" served me well. The show did go on, and I got through the weekend. But I was ever so glad each night to get safely home and put my arms around my huge furry friend, Hilarry. I only wish I had stuck it out through the end of the dog obedience course. Hilarry was a playful handful at almost 80 pounds by now and strong!! She literally dragged me around on our walks instead of heel, heel, heeling by my side. I never realized how much time and repetition it took to go over and over the commands until they were mastered. I flunked! Hilarry jumped up and crashed down the driveway fence wanting to follow us in the car. She demolished the infamous barstool Hudson had stood on leaving chunks of foam and black plastic all over the house. The living room door was swollen and couldn't shut tight, so sometimes when the kids were eating dinner in front of the TV, she would burst through the door, running to gobble up the kid's hamburgers like she was passing through a drive through. I probably had no business getting such a big dog, but I loved the way people moved to the side when she came their way … she was intimidating, when she wasn't being such a fun mess at home.

Well, the "key" episode, along with the constant fear and anxiety of being watched, finally took its toll on me. I never realized before how important a sense of security and safety is to the human spirit … psychologists say that "security" is number one of the four basic needs for women. I believe it. I was not made to live like this. I needed a retreat—a place to go where I could relax and restore my depleted reserves. Sunday, I confided in close friends and told them that I needed a safe place to secretly escape to where I could get some counseling and support. They agreed, and I called my longtime friends, Steve and Char from Mokena, south of Chicago. Back in 1985, they invited Hudson and Dawn to come stay with them for the six weeks right after my separation, hoping to give us the time and space to reconcile our marriage. They were extraordinary Christian people whom God placed in my life—a committed friendship I didn't earn or deserve. They opened wide the doors of hospitality to me. Arrangements were made for friends to take care of my children and dog (guess who? Yes, the "good" Ms. Phyllis). I took the Amtrak and came up for a week of "retreat": taking quiet meditative walks in the forest preserve as I enjoyed the changing of the fall leaves. I read inspirational books, engaged in normal family conversations that were not about me and my crises, and indulged in Chicago deep dish pizza. One of my former pastors gave me counsel and reassured me that our God is faithful. Our time together renewed my spiritual resolve to continue to trust God even during these hard times. I returned from my secret fall break ready to battle on.

I was learning what it meant to experience abiding JOY, not temporal happiness, which is usually based on pleasant circumstances. When my mother was sick, I gave her a small gift—a wooden plaque with these words painted on it: "JOY is not the absence of suffering, but the presence of God." How true!

If "What Women Want" is security, then financial security is what they really, really want. I began to feel the financial stress from being self-employed with seasonal work. I had to rely on good health (both physical and mental), energy, and opportunity to be able to produce income. If any event interrupted that trifecta, it could send me into a private economic recession.

The rape was just such an event.

The good people of Alexandria reached out to help me:

- YWCA Board members gave me a cash gift to buy food and immediate necessities.
- Someone helped me apply for compensation from the *Crime Victims Reparation Board*.
- Someone brought me to a non-profit to apply for reduced counseling for the children.
- Jack Mertens, owner of Owl Grocery, regularly brought us "barely expired but still good" food.
- Our church helped feed huge Hilarry with food scraps from potluck supper.
- Some anonymous person stuck a 22-cent stamp on an envelope and mailed a scrap of paper to me with these priceless words scrawled on it:

> *"The will of God will not lead you where*
> *the grace of God cannot keep you."*

(Paraphrase of Billy Graham's quote cited before.)

I would look often at that little piece of paper taped to my refrigerator and ask myself these questions:

1. Are my circumstances right now part of "God's Will"?
2. Did He allow these events to happen to me?

3. Is He still in control?
4. Is all this still a part of His "wonderful" plan for my life?
5. Is He still "causing ALL things to work together for GOOD to those who love God, to those who are called according to His purpose"? (Romans 8:28 *emphasis mine*)

My answers were always affirmative. Then, I had to logically conclude that if God has allowed these to come into my life, then He would also give me **Re-** as my companion for this journey— His gift of **GRACE** to give me the ability to stay the course.

> "His WILL won't lead me, where His GRACE can't keep me!"

It was simple. It was clear. It wasn't a "holy scripture," but it was a biblical truth incapsulated in a few easy-to-hang-onto words. I didn't even know until recently that the saying was a paraphrase of a quote from Evangelist Billy Graham … no wonder there was comforting wisdom in those words!

We can never underestimate the impact our ever so small contribution of time, money, or thoughtfulness can have on another needy human being—given in the spirit and love of Christ.

Paid In Full

One afternoon, months after my event, I received a phone call from Dick Ayres—the gentleman who came over to get my children the night of the rape. He was a church elder and a successful businessman. He asked if he could come over to my house and "talk business" with me. I didn't know exactly what that meant, but I knew I needed all the business help I could get. When Mr. Ayres came over, he asked me if I could pull out my bills and list for him all the debts that I currently owed:

- The mortgage was past due, along with my utility and phone bill
- A Sears credit card used for school clothes and supplies … a gas credit card, both had balances due
- Payments on a lease/purchase of an electric typewriter to type up fitness brochures and manuals
- Medical bills for myself and the children

The process of bringing out all my debts was rather humbling. I currently had no means to be able to pay them and most likely would just incur more debts in the future and get further behind. I had no power to change my situation; it seemed hopeless. Mr. Ayres agreed that they were all my legal obligation to pay. However, he was here as my advocate, before God, to clear my case and free me from all my debts. My debts would be "paid in full" as a gift from my church family. They wanted me to have a fresh financial start from this point forward, so I could focus on getting better. Mr. Ayres totaled up the debts, which came to a huge number in my mind, pulled out the big church business checkbook, and made out a check to me for that exact amount. He instructed me to deposit the check in my personal account and pay all my creditors so that I owed nothing. He prayed with me and then left.

What just happened? I collapsed onto the kitchen picnic bench is disbelief, still holding the check. ALL my debts were now "paid in full," and it was a gift. I didn't work to earn this money to pay off my own debts- someone else worked for me and gave this money to me as a "free love gift." All I had to do was hold out my hand to **re**ceive the gift. I was forgiven my debts. I was financially free. Sitting on that hard bench, I felt emotionally weightless, even light-hearted. **Re**lieved. Grateful. Hopeful... *Déjà vu!* I had that strange feeling that I had already experienced spiritually what was happening in the present physical realm. Yes!

> *"For the wages of sin is death, but the free gift of God is eternal life in Christ Jesus our Lord"* (Romans 6:23).

I felt like I was back sitting on that "couch in Conroe," two years before on November 12, 1985, when I first experienced the miracle of having all my debts wiped out and declared to be "paid in full." That was when I was **re**deemed: bought back and brought back into a right relationship with God, paid for with the blood of Jesus Christ. I admitted I was penniless and had nothing

I could offer God. Only at that point of brokenness, **re**cognizing my *spiritual* poverty, could I **re**ceive the heavenly gift.

But just how did I find myself back in Conroe, Texas, where I had lived almost ten years ago?

There is no logical answer.

Only God's GPS could have led me to this crossroad.

Chapter 15

MY PERFECT FIVE-MINUTE TESTIMONY

WHEN LIFE ISN'T clearly defined, it's always helpful to pull out the reliable Merriam-Webster Dictionary: Testimony: "a public profession of a religious experience."[20]

> Evangelism: "comes from the Greek word: *euangelion* from *eu* meaning 'good' and *angelion* meaning 'message or news.' 'Good News.'"[21]

> Evangelical: "3) *emphasizing salvation by faith in the atoning death of Jesus Christ through personal conversion, the authority of scripture, and the importance of preaching as contrasted with ritual.*"[22]

Re- *and* Me

So, in some Evangelical circles, it is popular to "*share your testimony of the Good News.*" You can write it down and practice presenting it in under five minutes following the three-point sermon formula:

1. Your life before you met Jesus Christ
2. How you knew you needed Him
3. Your life after you met Jesus Christ

I did this and shared my story on several occasions. Here is a version of my original testimony:

"My road of life started at conception when I was created with the unique DNA that maps out the characteristics that I inherited from my family genes. In my family, autoimmune diseases, alcoholism, and depression are prevalent. What I also inherited is that human 'nature of sin'.

> *That nature of sin, namely, my claim to my right to myself, entered into the human race through one man (Adam) … The nature of sin is not immorality and wrongdoing, but the nature of self-realization which leads us to say 'I am my own god.' This nature may exhibit itself in proper morality, or in improper immorality, but it always has a common basis—my claim to my right to myself*[23]

> *(Oswald Chambers).*

That pretty much summed up me … my-my-my. It was all about me—I was a talented ambitious overachiever, and I relished being in control. In my mind, I truly was my own god.

Like most WASPs (White Anglo-Saxon Protestants) from the 60s, I grew up attending my traditional Presbyterian church with my family on Sunday mornings. We had to polish our shoes on Saturday night. We set out our church clothes for the next day. I had a sprinkling baptism as an infant, went to Sunday school and Vacation Bible School as a child, and attended a special course in seventh grade called Communicate Class to study the church doctrines and be able to participate in communion. We always said grace before meals, celebrated Christmas with lights, trees, lots of food, and presents. We went to church service on Easter Sunday wearing our new spring outfits. I would get emotional and cry on Easter mornings when the choir sang the hymn, "Christ Our Lord is Risen Today." By all accounts, I was a Christian.

In eighth grade, I auditioned for the Dallas Civic Ballet, and my number one priority became dance. I had rehearsals on Sundays, so I slept in and quit attending morning church services. My younger brother got into some trouble as a juvenile delinquent, and when my mother tried to get help from our church, they were out of touch and not helpful, so my parents quit church too. My high school boyfriend was involved in Young Life, a non-denominational Evangelical organization. Every December, they went to Colorado for a YL ski trip. I had never been to the mountains or skiing … as a contracted professional ballet dancer, I wasn't allowed to participate in risky activities where I might be injured. My senior year, I secretly joined my classmates for a 'Rocky Mountain high' experience without telling my director. Every night, there were fun meetings: singing with guitars, skits, and then the speaker would give 'The Talk' about Jesus. The last night was always 'The Cross Talk' about Jesus's suffering on behalf of us sinners and our **re**sponse to that. We were invited to pray and 'accept Jesus Christ as our personal Lord and Savior.'

I **re**membered my childhood faith. I certainly wanted to be sure I was saved and would go to heaven. However, I was not quite ready for Him to be my Lord, the other half of the deal. That would be too scary to give Him that control—I'd decide on that later. But I decided Jesus could be my Savior. So, in keeping with my 'conversion,' I began to live 'the Christian lifestyle,' doing all the right things: I attended Sunday services at a Bible church, went to Bible studies, memorized Bible verses, had a daily biblical devotional time through my years after high school graduation and through college.

After college, I got married in a Bible church to my high school boyfriend in a very 'Christian Evangelical' ceremony. Just to be sure I was obedient, after I got married, I decided to have a 'believer's baptism' as an adult—a full immersion dunking—and was given a certificate to mark the occasion. My husband went into full time ministry with Young Life in Conroe, Texas, and I helped serve in that ministry. My husband went to graduate theological training in Dallas and Chicago, and then we moved to Alexandria, Louisiana, where he became the youth pastor in a church. I helped lead the high school girls in church activities. Eventually, he left his church position, switched to counseling, and worked as a medic. I helped women stay fit with aerobic classes. We had two beautiful children together. That's how I changed to start living 'the Christian life.'"

(THIS was my five-minute version of "MY truth," and I believed it sincerely.)

Five Minutes Up Already? Wait! It's Long & Complicated!

Oops! Did I leave out the part about my infidelities, the voices in my head, the butcher knife to my wrist, my friend's children getting hurled out of bed and down flights of stairs? Like I said, it's complicated. Long and complicated. Well, that was my neat and tidy testimony. Here's my real, and real messy story.

So, this next part of "my story for His glory" is hard to retell … could I just skip this part? It doesn't frame me in a very flattering light—I want people to like me and admire me, but to be honest, I am a "wretch" of a sinner. It's been much easier to tell the story of how I was innocently a victim of a serial rapist and how I got through that … I showed courage, **re**silience, and strength of character by the grace of God. But to be transparent and truthful and tell my friend **Re**-'s story of "Amazing Grace" … just how lost I was before I was found is hard to admit. If

I don't take the gloves off and paint a real "before" picture of Becky, how can God get the glory for His miracle of **Re**-Becky? I was that one stray sheep wandering off. My good shepherd left the others to come find me!!

I had a lot of lies and negative self-talk going on in my head all the time from about seventh grade on. To say I was a "hot mess" is understating the facts. Not unusual for a ballerina, I developed eating disorders—anorexia during high school that morphed into bulimorexia during college … a secret and shameful pattern. I read that Jane Fonda and Princess Diana had the same problems, but it didn't make me feel any better to be in such fine company. Clinically, the anorexia eating disorder is about control, but is often accompanied with sexuality issues; a high percentage of female sufferers have child sexual abuse history. For me, age seven-in Iowa. My girlfriend, Donna, and I were tied up and molested in a cornfield by some teenage boys—one of them the sheriff's son. My mother tried to have them arrested, but it was futile. Also, many anorexics have "father issues"—my father was smitten with the buxom Dallas Cowboy Cheerleaders, and I was his flat-chested ballerina girl. I disappointed him.

Back to the negative self-talk. There was something more at play here. The negative self-talk and strong thoughts filling my head became more dominant through the years, and I began to realize that I was a spectator, not a participant, in these conversations. The voices told me: "I'm a failure; I should run away; I should end it all; God isn't going to help me; God doesn't want me to be happy."

I had a frightening episode one evening in Dallas while we were in graduate school. I was in the kitchen chopping vegetables for dinner when I inexplicably couldn't control my hand—another force was bringing my hand over to chop my wrist, and only with a concerted effort could I throw the knife down and run out of our mobile home, scared and perplexed. I never watched any of the popular supernatural horror films that came out in the '70s: *The Exorcist I & II*, *Whatever Happened to Rosemary's Baby*, and *Carrie*. Everywhere, interest in the occult was on the rise. I began to suspect that my struggles were of a dark spiritual nature, but I abandoned that notion due to the cultural backlash within the conservative Christian movement, which dismissed much of the satanic supernatural phenomena as "Hollywood propaganda" and sensationalism.

I felt like my mental health was starting to fragment. An appointment was set up with one of my husband's professors at Dallas Theological Seminary, Dr. Haddon Robinson, to see if he could discern what was really going on. Was this all about my struggle with my passion for dance trying to make it my "god," or about my eating disorders and infidelities, our marriage tension and financial problems, or yet something else? He told me that with just one counseling appointment, he couldn't be sure, but he didn't believe that any of those were at the root of this fight. He sensed that, "I was in a deep spiritual battle, face-to-face with the God of the universe."

Directly in a battle with **the Big G**! Oh my gosh!! Now that did scare me. Dr. Robinson was the only one who even came close to the truth, and the Lord placed him in my path at just the right moment ... a few months later, he left Dallas to become president of Denver Seminary, and we left Dallas to seek help.

This next part of my testimony would be easy to gloss over and give the sanitized version of what happened next, but I'm compelled to tell the "truth, the whole truth, so help me God."

My Joliet "Prison"
August 1979

We decided to go up to Joliet, Illinois, for an extended visit with our mentors from DTS—Pat and Linda, a young couple who had moved back home after graduation to start a church plant. We needed their counsel about our marriage and future. Besides pastoring the home church, Pat was in partnership with some other men in the church, purchasing fixer-uppers and flipping them. We were shocked to drive up and see the gorgeous two-story historical home they lived in ... one of their better deals! It was late, and since we were tired from the trip, we had light conversation and were shown upstairs to the guest bedroom. All three bedrooms were upstairs; we shared a wall with Pat and Linda's master bedroom; they shared the wall with their children's bedroom; and we all shared the small communal hallway outside our doors that led to the wide and winding staircase down to the family room. We slept in, but they were up early with their two children, a little four-year-old girl and two-and-a-half-year-old boy.

My Perfect Five-Minute Testimony

When we came down for coffee and breakfast, the kids were already finished and in the other room playing, but Pat and Linda were still discussing the strange occurrence in their home. Their little girl had apparently sleep-walked all the way downstairs to the kitchen during the night. She opened the pantry door and pulled everything down off the shelves, emptying boxes of cereal and syrup all over the floor, spreading the mixture everywhere, and then went back upstairs to bed unaware of what she had done. They said she was a sweet obedient girl and had never done anything like this before. We were not even parents yet, so we weren't knowledgeable enough to make judgments. This behavior was repeated the next night and the next and the next: rice, pasta, shortening, syrup, flour, sugar, spices—mixed and smeared on the cabinets and floors.

The children slept in standard adult height twin beds, one on each side of the room with eight feet or so of wooden floor space between them. This night around midnight, we all heard a loud "thump" and crying ... Linda jumped out of bed and quickly went in the kids' room to find her daughter lying in a heap on the floor ... four feet from her bed. It is not uncommon for young children to roll off the bed during the night and slip onto the floor ... but NOT four feet from the bed. This event happened again and again, and then the little boy was also "hurled" out of bed. They would jump up and go into their room as soon as they heard the noise, maybe 20 seconds later, and find their child already across the room on the floor—not a place they could have rolled from the bed to that spot "naturally." Other *unnatural* things began to take place. Next, the children started tumbling down the stairs, but again it was more like getting "pushed" down the stairs. I went to the forest preserve to jog through the trail and was chased by a swarm of bees for several miles. We were continuing our marriage counseling with our hosts, but our nerves were on edge from the lack of sleep and waiting for the next strange event to happen.

My husband and I decided to take a road trip over to Iowa and up to the far northwest corner to the little town of Storm Lake—where I grew up. Midwesterners can be hard to get to know at first as compared to overtly friendly Southerners, but once you have made a friend, you are friends on the deepest level for life. I reconnected with some of the families I knew there—my parents had kept in touch through Christmas cards. The town was every bit as idyllic as I remembered, and sadly, the large house with the cornfield behind it was still there to bring back hurtful memories.

While we were gone, our hosts had been visiting with some old missionary friends who were home on furlough from the mission field. The night that we returned, our host's little girl was hurled out of bed several times, and the next morning, their little boy was again pushed down the stairs. Fortunately, the children had not been injured ... yet. The incidents had ceased while we were on our trip and then began again when we returned.

Pat and Linda had described these bizarre events to their missionary friends who said that they had witnessed demonic control and possession in the countries they had served and

My Perfect Five-Minute Testimony

told our hosts that surely this must be from a demonic source. Unbeknownst to me, there were further meetings with the missionaries, our hosts, and other church leaders. All of this built up to the big "showdown." This night, upstairs in the bedroom, my husband told me that some of the leaders were coming by to pick us up to go "pray" together. He left to go downstairs to wait for them, and I was left alone—but then, I wasn't "alone." I went into a frenzy like a caged squirrel who was caught ... I went into the bathroom and grabbed a bottle of aspirin and began to down them, unable to stop—better dead than delivered. The upstairs side bedroom window had no screen and was open, with the concrete driveway right below. Unseen forces were pushing me from behind, and with what was left of my will, I desperately clung onto the framework to keep from being thrown out the window. Just then, I saw lights from a car coming up the driveway, and thankfully, my husband ran upstairs to get me. They drove us over to an empty house being remodeled to meet the other men who had already gathered and were sitting in a circle on folding chairs.

Maybe you have seen some of those movies and are waiting to hear a juicy description of gravely voices, spinning heads, writhing convulsions, and green vomit. Or you have read the biblical account of Jesus casting out the Legion of demons from the naked crazy man walking among the tombs and remember how the demons then possessed a herd of swine and threw them off the cliff, drowning them in the sea below (reference to Matthew 8:28–34; Mark 5:1–20).

Sorry to disappoint. My deliverance was comparatively tame and resembled more of a somber prayer gathering. The men simply went from person to person around the circle, and each one humbly confessed before the Lord his shortcomings and hidden sins, asking for forgiveness. Then they prayed to be filled with a special measure of the Holy Spirit and asked for discernment and wisdom. During this time, I sat rigidly in my chair, arms folded, staring down to the floor, focused on a microscopic piece of paper lying there. It was my turn now, and I was literally in the "hot seat." The lead pastor began to ask me questions, probing into my past, looking for a point where I could have opened myself up to demonic activity:

1. Had I ever done drugs or been around the drug culture? — NO
2. Had I exposed myself to witchcraft, incantations, spells? — NO
3. Had I ever gone to a fortune teller, a reader of tarot cards? — NO
4. Did I follow astrology columns, read zodiac books, etc.? — NO
5. Did I practice transcendental meditation-yoga meditation? — NO
6. Was I ever under the influence of any cults: Christian Science, Scientology, Pseudo-Christian Cults? — NO
7. Was I addicted to pornography? Did I view or engage in deviant sexual behavior? — NO

My Perfect Five-Minute Testimony

I stayed in a stubborn trance-like state, focused on that speck of paper on the floor, but I could hardly hear their questions because all the while, the voices in my head were screaming out profanities not even in my vocabulary and telling me, "Don't listen. Don't believe them. They are liars." I heard the pastor's last question, and it jarred a forgotten memory from long ago:

8. Have you ever played Ouija Board, participated in seances, or tried to summon spirits back from the dead? — **YES!**

Yes! The memory came back to me crystal clear. During middle school, slumber parties were popular. We would dance to the Beach Boys and the Beatles, eat M&Ms, play card games, *and* play with the Ouija Board where "spirits" would guide us to answer questions like who our next boyfriend would be. We also would sit in a circle, and one girl would lead us in a séance … our favorite one was "bringing Marilyn Monroe back from the dead" after her tragic decapitating car accident. It was all just innocent fun and games to me. None of us really believed any of it was real, just a big joke. But one night, one party was different and very real for me.

I had a girlfriend, Suzi, who had just moved into a luxury apartment, and her parents rented out the adjacent empty apartment for our slumber party. We were having a great time and decided to light candles and have a séance. This time, I went into a trance and had an out-of-body experience. My eyes were wide open, but I couldn't speak, respond, or move—even when my girlfriends shook me and carried me to the bathtub and poured cold water on me. I could "watch" this all happening to me from a vantage point somewhere above my body. Unable to wake me from this trance, some girls started to cry, thinking I was in a coma and went next door to get the parents. When they came over, I "woke up" and told the girls I was just a great actress who could maintain and not break character, but inside I knew that couldn't be true.

Months later, I went to another slumber party over at another girlfriend's house where they also were having seances … I was so scared that I told them I was sick and called my parents to pick me up. I never told anyone about the out-of-body experience and never went to another séance.

That was it! That was the entry point of demonic influence. The séance was a game to me, but Satan took it seriously. Evidently, my eating disorder became another "hook" for a stronger demonic control because even though it was psychologically defined as a "disorder," it involved the problem of binging, a habitual sin biblically known as "gluttony." My poor self-esteem was fodder for the three named demonic spirits called out, "Failure," "Runaway," and "Destruction," and my rebellion over God's control over my life allowed them to burrow deeper into my soul. When I finally did confess and pray and ask to be freed from this prison and the power of these evil spirits, there was a tangible "heavy weight" that lifted off my chest, as the unseen spirits arose and left me. Because it was late Saturday night, or more correctly early Sunday morning, the missionary said that I would probably be exhausted and sleep all day.

The Truth Shall Set You Free

Not so! A few hours later I woke up, eager to go to Sunday morning church service at the home of Steve and Char. I couldn't believe the startling difference inside my head from pre- to post-deliverance: I had a completely clear head with NO voices—beautifully free from all the inner conversations of the spirits influencing me with their unrelenting self-destructive words, which had become louder and more confusing the past few years as I gave into my bitterness and anger. I could finally sing through a song or hymn in church without my throat swelling up and stopping me. Satan must hate worship of the true God. I could sit outside after the church service and observe nature and just *be*—full of peace and quiet in my head.

This dramatic overnight change and total **re**lease is the talking point in distinguishing between a legitimate diagnosis of *mental illness*—schizophrenia, psychosis, multiple personality disorder—and a genuine demonic deliverance. The latter is a spiritual problem which results in an instantaneous change without medication, medical procedures, or long-term counseling and intervention. Never having been inside another person's mind, I assumed the conversations going on were just "me talking to me." There was never any outer or audible verbalization to distinguish a thought or a "voice" as not being my own and coming from another source.

In so many ways, I felt childlike: starting over, **re**discovering who "me" was, without the voices trying to influence and destroy me.

From August of 1979 until June of 1981 when we moved from Joliet to Alexandria, I lived quietly in my new normal—giving up ballet performance to become a mom.

To symbolize the dramatic change in my life and in understanding God's power in **re**naming those He chooses:

Abram became *Abraham*

Sarai became *Sarah*

Jacob became *Israel*

Simon became (Apostle) *Peter*

I asked to be called by my given name, **Rebecca**, and not my nickname, Becky. I loved that my name was biblical, although it had the Latin Vulgate spelling. My mother named me after the heroine in the book, *Rebecca of Sunnybrook Farm*.

The name, "*Rebekah*," comes from the Hebrew verb "*rbq*," meaning "to bind," or "tied up" and "secured," such as the tying up of cattle for their protection to keep them from wandering off[24]. Within this name lies the notion that individuals are placed together by something higher or smarter than they.

God was reeling in my ropes to bind me close to His heart for my protection.

Chapter 16

THE BIRTH OF RE-BECKY

1981–1985

"**Re**becca" was "tied up" in the busyness of life in Alexandria for the next four years, but **Re-** securely held onto the ropes, warning me to "be of sober spirit, be on the alert. Your adversary, the devil, prowls around like a roaring lion, seeking someone to devour." (1 Peter 5:8). **Re-** tried to warn me, but I stretched the ropes out to the max.

Satan is real, as I had already learned first-hand. He is all about pride ... he desired to be God, not a servant of God. Hmmm ... sounds like me; I wanted Jesus to be my Savior but not my Lord. The enemy's most slick temptation is called the "pride of life" (1 John 2:16). Loving the world becomes more important than loving the Lord. The problem is that the pride of life can look "good" from afar: taking care of a home; raising healthy, smart, and successful children; 12-step personal improvement and self-actualization programs; using your gifts and talents to help others; receiving recognition for your accomplishments; fulfilling your career ambitions. I was busy with these "good" things, but the temptation was that they could lead to arrogance, boasting, self-sufficiency, and presumption. Like my sister Eve, I was deceived and fell into the trap.

"Sin will take you farther than you want to go,

Keep you longer than you want to stay,

And cost you more than you want to pay"[25]

I warned you this story would be long and real messy! We all have things in our past we **re**gret and that we are ashamed to **re**count—I have many, but when the Lord **re**plays the video of my life, I have one night that I will especially cringe to watch...

> *"For we must all appear before the judgment seat of Christ, so that each one may be **re**compensed for his deeds in the body, according to what he has done, whether good or bad" (2 Corinthians 5:10).*

When it comes to temptations to sin, we often **re**lapse back into old familiar patterns. I did. I was a mother of young children, leading aerobic classes in the evenings at a health club to a mixed crowd of men and women. Afterwards, a group of the class participants would hang out and chat for a bit at the smoothie bar. I enjoyed the attention I got from being a top-tier teacher, the freedom to talk with adults while my kids were in club childcare, and the excuse that my husband worked too much and wasn't home enough to pay attention to me. Everyone knows where this is going … the trap! One of the single guys lived a few blocks from me—I put the kids down to bed one night when my husband was on the overnight shift, and I went over there and stayed for over an hour while they were still home asleep! Inexcusable … I left my children unattended, by themselves! *Cringe!* Understandably, this was the last straw on the back of my tenuous marriage. My husband confronted me—informed me he was filing for separation/divorce and told me I was to pack and leave.

The Couch In Conroe

Remorseful, distraught, and suicidal after that confrontation, I got into my car with nothing but my purse and his loaded revolver from the cabinet over the refrigerator and left my home in Alexandria driving north on the highway up to Shreveport, maybe heading up and over to Dallas? To family? To Joyce? I don't know. I pulled over to a pay phone to make a last desperate phone call back home and then pulled off the road later to fire the gun to be sure it worked. I was a hopeless failure and felt like there was no way back for me. Then for *some mysterious reason*, it came to me that I should go see my dancer friend, Jan, in Conroe whom I hadn't seen in years. She understands me; she has known me since I first married … maybe she could give me a reason to keep going. I turned the car around and drove south.

I knocked on the door, and Jan's husband, Eddie, answered. Jan wasn't home—she was at a dance conference in Dallas and wouldn't be home until much later. She was not there. What's the point? I should just make this easy on everyone. I drove to the corner gas station, bought a yellow spiral notebook and took a dirt road into the piney woods and parked. There I wrote my suicide note. A person who has never had bouts of depression or thoughts of taking their own life to escape the present pain cannot understand the state of mind you find yourself in. My grandmother, Mamoo, was just such a person, and she could never understand or forgive my brother Larry for shooting himself. The way she handled it was just to be angry at him for leaving his family and being so selfish. I knew she was wrong. When a person is in that state of darkness, they are convinced that they have messed up so badly or have been such a disappointment that the most "unselfish" thing they can do is not be here anymore to cause problems to others. It is a sad lie.

On the cover of my spiral notebook (which I still have and **re**purposed—minus the actual note that I tore up later)—I thoughtfully wrote a note to the police: "—Sorry for the mess—please inform my husband, he is wondering. The contents are private for my husband to read" and then I had written down all his contact information. Inside I wrote my note to my husband, said again how sorry I was for all the hurt I had caused AND that "this was best because Hudson and Dawn deserved to have a better mommy than me." I was convinced that this was the most logical thing I could do. Of course, I was sobbing, lamenting that my life had come to this. The Dutch Catholic Priest and Theologian, Henri Nouwen, describes the struggle this way:

> *"The voice of despair says, 'I sin over and over again. After endless promises to myself and others to do better next time, I find myself back again in the old dark places. Forget about trying to change. I have tried for years. It didn't work, and it never will work. It is better that I get out of people's way, be forgotten, no longer around, dead.' This strangely attractive voice takes all uncertainties away and puts an end to the struggle. It speaks unambiguously for the darkness and offers a clear-cut negative identity."*[26]

With the loaded gun ready to go, right next to me, I cried out to the Lord and asked Him why He hadn't answered my prayers, why I kept struggling and failing in life. I told Him I was tired of trying, and I just wanted to be free and be with Him in a few moments. Oh yeah, I forgot to mention that my Little 2-Letter Friend, **Re-**, was also right next to me, sitting in my passenger seat. She intervened right before that final, "NOW" moment. God's **grace** planted this one strong thought in my mind, doubtful and hopeful at the same time: "Maybe you're NOT going to see God in just a moment ... maybe there's a reason He hasn't answered ... maybe you should wait and go back to Jan's before you give up." I **re**jected the lies about myself that Satan wanted me to believe and instead, by God's **grace**, I listened to her voice as Nouwen describes it:

> *"But Jesus came to open my ears to another voice that says, 'I am your God; I have molded you with my own hands, and I love what I have made. I love you with a love that has no limits because I love you as I am loved. Do not run away from me. ... Please do not say that I have given up on you, that I cannot stand you anymore, that there is no way back. It is not true. ... Do not judge yourself. Do not condemn yourself. Do not reject yourself. Let my love touch the deepest, most hidden corners of your heart and **re**veal to you your own beauty, a beauty that you have lost sight of, but that will become visible to you again in the light of my mercy. Come, come, let me wipe your tears, and let my mouth come close to your ear and say to you, 'I love you, I love you, I love you.'"*[27]

"Hi there, Becky," Jan said as she opened the door. "What's going on? Eddie told me you had come by earlier," Jan questioned as she let me in, knowing that something awful must have happened for me to show up unannounced—years since my last visit. I walked in carrying my purse and my loaded gun close to me, and she invited me to come sit on her couch to talk. I told her that I didn't want her to come near the couch or to talk me out of what I needed to do but to just be my "friend" and help take care of the aftermath. She listened to everything about my spiritual struggles, my marriage problems, and my most recent failure. When I came to the end of my soliloquy, she asked if I would let her do one last thing for me. Could she call a pastor in Houston she followed on Christian television to see if he could talk with me?

Oh great, I thought, here are Jan and her "charismatic" Christian TV friends who I think are off track. Yes, that would be OK, but I told her he wasn't going to change my mind. She called the Houston office of Pastor Mickey Bonner, a southern Baptist evangelist. His secretary answered and said that the pastor was in the office only to pick up some materials on his way to go out of town to a conference. Jan explained the circumstances and said that it was urgent that we speak to him. The lady said he only had about 45 minutes before he had to leave. I don't know why I said I would talk to this guy … I didn't even respect the theology of this type of charismatic preacher.

Pastor Bonner started right in with his own set of questions for me. His line of inquiry involved going back into my family history and my own personal experience, discovering generational patterns of sin. Once those were identified, he asked me to pray with him over the phone, to **re**nounce each of those strongholds in my life and **re**pent of them: the sin of the spirit of seduction, of negative confession and suicide, of

rejection from the womb, and of self will and self-centeredness. Following his lead, I prayed to God, confessing that Jesus is the way and the truth and the life and that no one can come to the Father but by Him. I asked for the forgiveness that only Jesus can give and for Him to take over my life totally—I **re**linquished all control to Him. After he said "Amen," a heavy darkness floated upward out of my heart—a sensation I had once before, and I handed the phone back to Jan.

Jan followed up the conversation with the secretary and jotted down the details of the conference in Corpus Christi coming up Thursday–Saturday. She said that Pastor Bonner wanted to meet me there to follow up and would have a place for me to stay. Jan hung up the phone, and I handed over the gun. Instantaneously, I was changed! Minutes ago, I was despondent, determined to give up and take my own life. Now, inexplicably I had hope and was determined to do as the pastor suggested and "aggressively pursue righteousness." I was going to follow Jesus—go back to my family and face the consequences whatever they would be. It was Tuesday. Jan and I talked for hours over the next few days and studied passages in the Bible together. She couldn't get over the sudden positive changes in me, and in fun, she started calling me "**Re**-Becky." I left Jan's house on Thursday morning with nothing but hope and hugs and the peanut butter sandwich lunch she had packed for me. All I had in my wallet were two credit cards—Sears and a gas card. I made the almost five-hour drive down to Corpus and located the Hershey Hotel on North Shoreline Drive. It was

4:00 p.m. I asked the front desk concierge where the 7:00 p.m. Mickey Bonner conference was to be held, and he directed me to the third floor, to the "Nueces Ballroom."

In The Ballroom With The Lead Pipe

The chairs were set up, but the room was empty of people. I sat in the first aisle seat on the fourth row with the Bible Jan gave to me, pulled out the yellow spiral notebook, and began to journal:

"Praise you Jesus for leading me here … I praise You for the outpouring of my soul and mind on the way down here to reveal the truth about myself and my problem to me and prepare me to receive YOUR message & word tonight. God—help me to see myself—in all my sin, depravity, and wickedness and to fully realize perhaps for the first time, my true condition, that I am totally unable to pull myself out of sin or to keep from running to it, and I cannot have life—physical life and spiritual life without Your absolute power and control of my will—I need a new will—Yours. My old will only knows how to listen to self & sin. I am desperate—there absolutely are no other answers, explanations, or help for my life and sanity other than the redeeming power of Your grace. Sin has overwhelmed me—I'm sold out to it—set me free from its bondage to serve You. Fill me with your

Holy Spirit each moment and press out the voices where evil is drawn. Change me profoundly as a totally new creature in Christ."

"*New creature in Christ?*" I knew that Bible verse was somewhere in here; found it: *(2 Corinthians 5:17–6:2)*

*"Therefore if anyone is in Christ, he is a new creature; the old things passed away; behold, new things have come. Now all these things are from God, who **re**conciled us to Himself through Christ ... He made Him who knew no sin to be sin on our behalf, so that we might become the righteousness of God in Him. (6:1&2), And working together with Him, we also urge you not to receive the grace of God in vain for He says,*

'AT THE ACCEPTABLE TIME I LISTENED TO YOU, AND ON THE DAY OF SALVATION I HELPED YOU.' Behold, now is "THE ACCEPTABLE TIME," behold, now is "THE DAY OF SALVATION"

There it was, **NOW** ... the power of the word NOW—at the exact precise mysterious moment—at God's chosen and acceptable time, God listened to me and helped me ... NOW is the DAY of salvation! Continuing my journal:

The Birth of Re-Becky

*"Lord—is it possible, after all these years, that I have just had the conversion experience & really & truly and finally—being broken down to call out on Your name alone and your blood—perhaps could sin have so infiltrated & dominated my life that I had never truly seen myself as a hopeless sinner in utter need of help—change—hope—salvation & been willing to **re**pent & do anything to turn away from my old way of life & sins—to have You.*

Is this the first time ever You have truly come in & sat down on the throne of my life? Oh Jesus, at last, are You going to come into me & sup w/me & live next to me in fellowship & fill me with Your presence? Please say yes! You have been knocking & beating on my door for so long & now I have just finally opened up my heart to let you in—we've been talking thru the peephole all these years!!"

Tuesday Nov. 12—I became a Christian, *a real believer—on telephone—transformed—Mickey Bonner—True* **Re***pentance—*

Oh Lord—thank You for saving me— You had to go to so much trouble to pursue me all these years. Thank You for never giving up on me—I have no fears now—of going … wherever You send me—I'll go; I'm Yours. At last we're talking face-to-face and not thru the peephole. **Re***store me to wholeness in Jesus."*

Re- *and* Me

I couldn't have been more shocked than if I had been hit over the head with a lead pipe in that ballroom! Who would believe me? That after all the years of trying hard on my own to live my religious, self-righteous Christian life, I only just NOW was "born again" and became a true believer ... on the "couch in Conroe." How could this be?

Around 6:00 p.m., hotel staff began to come in to set up the water table and check microphones as attendees began to trickle in. Pastor Bonner came into the room just before 7:00 p.m. and began to dynamically preach and teach on his topic, "spiritual warfare." He was surrounded by groups of people at both the mid-session break and at the conclusion of the evening. I waited until almost everyone else had left before I approached Pastor Bonner and introduced myself:

"I'm the girl you talked to and prayed with on the phone a few days ago in Houston—Rebecca. You won't believe this—I just became a Christian that day!"

"It's about time—what took you so long?" he **re**sponded with enthusiasm. "I knew it when I finished praying with you because there was such a total **re**lease—that's why I asked you if this was the first time you had prayed to receive salvation."

"Why in darkness, Lord—why separated from the light of Your presence, why so long—time is quickly passing."

He introduced me to Mildred, a sweet woman maybe in her late 50s who was to be my host for the next few days. I got in my car and followed her as she led me to her fashionable condominium where she gave me food, lodging, and love for those next few days. By the close of the seminar Saturday afternoon—during the last group prayer time, I wrote in my spiral notebook:

> "In prayer time, answer from the Lord to go directly home— He is the mighty Counselor. **R**epent, ask forgiveness and face the situation, & tell of my conversion ... together w/ Jesus, I can face it & trust God to work it all out somehow."

Chapter 17

THE REFINER

"WORK IT ALL OUT SOMEHOW." Hmmm, how did that go for you, you're asking? Well, you already know, not so good. But "not so good" according to my limited perspective was still "good" according to God. **Re**member:

> *"And we know that God causes all things to work together for good to those who love God, to those who are called according to His purpose"* (Romans 8:28).

What would my version of "good" have been? Here's how I would have worked all things together: I would go back to Alexandria and have my husband embrace my "just got saved story," miraculously forgive me, drop the divorce proceedings, and keep our little family glued together with lots of counseling. I would not have to experience the wrath of a revengeful ex-husband, the trauma of surviving an attack by a serial rapist, and the ongoing damage to my children from a contentious custody battle. But that version was not to be God's will for me.

How do I understand this? Elisabeth Elliot, the wife of the martyred missionary to Ecuador, Jim Elliot, wrote a book, *Through Gates of Splendor*, about the five missionaries who gave their lives in 1956 while in the jungle trying to share the Gospel with the Waodani tribe. In her Epilogue II, January 1996, she makes some profound statements about God's will, having experienced even more tragedies in life (she lost her second husband to cancer only a few years after their marriage), and yet she continued to trust God and traveled the world as a renown Christian speaker, author, and radio host. She shares her immense wisdom with these words:

> *"God is God. If He is God, He is worthy of my worship and my service. I will find rest nowhere but in His will, and that will is infinitely, immeasurably, unspeakably beyond my largest notions of what He is up to ... God is God. I dethrone Him in my heart if I demand that He act in ways that satisfy my idea of justice. There is unbelief, there is even rebellion, in the attitude that says, 'God has no right to do this ... unless. ... I believe with all my heart that God's story has a happy ending. Julian of Norwich wrote, 'All shall be well, and all shall be well,*

and all manner of thing shall be well.' But not yet, not necessarily yet. It takes faith to hold on to that in the face of the great burden of experience, which seems to prove otherwise. What God means by happiness and goodness is a far higher thing than we can conceive."[28]

Elisabeth is right, and God tells me:

"'For My thoughts are not your thoughts, nor are your ways My ways,' declares the Lord. For as the heavens are higher than the earth, so are My ways higher than your ways and My thoughts than your thoughts" (Isaiah 55:8-9).

God certainly did not do it my way, that is for sure. When I returned to Alexandria after the weekend of Mickey Bonner's "Spiritual Warfare" seminar, I was baptized by fire—under heavy attack, in the heat of battle, on the front lines, from day one. It was intense. It was a season of trials and tribulations for those next four years, from November '85 to September of '89. The first few trials were the natural consequences of my sinful choices that initiated the divorce process; rejected, homeless, jobless, penniless, childless. But after that, it escalated into a severe fiery ordeal, trial after trial, test after test, in every area of my life. Why had God allowed all this to happen to me? Is it true that, "God **re**deems all He allows?" Is there a purpose in the suffering that He allows? Gradually, I surrendered to the

Lord and said, **YES** to Him:

> **Y**ield to the Spirit
>
> **E**mbrace Grace
>
> **S**ubmit to God

The Lord was graciously taking me through His **re**fining process:

> *"I have **re**fined you, though not as silver; I have tested you in the furnace of affliction"* (Isaiah 48:10).

The brokenness I experienced on the couch in Conroe was just the beginning of His process of mining the precious silver and gold out of me. After He crushed me, He brought me back home ... but then threw me into the *crucible*, His fireproof melting pot, and placed me into the hot furnace.

Was my heart changed; was my conversion genuine?

> *"The crucible for silver and the furnace for gold, but the Lord tests the heart"* (Proverbs 17:3).

As He turned up the heat, the impurities of my character: pride, rebellion, self-centeredness, and **re**sentment began to float to the surface like dross:

> *"Remove the dross from the silver, and a silversmith can produce a vessel"* (Proverbs 25:4).

When I sat on the edge of the bathtub at Betsy's the morning after the rape and asked the Lord, "Hadn't I already been through enough trials already even before this?" His answer was "No!"

"All shall be well … and all manner of thing shall be well" (Julian of Norwich) but not yet, not necessarily yet.

He continued to test me.

Again and again.

He turned up the heat in this purification process.

He continued to skim off the dross in my life:

> *"And the words of the Lord are flawless, like silver purified in a crucible, like gold refined seven times"* (Psalm 12:6).

Seven times!

What is the goal of my **Refiner**?

What is the purpose for the suffering that the Lord sometimes allows in my life?

One purpose is that my way becomes His way:

> *"He knows the way that I take; when He has tested me, I will come forth as gold"* (Job 23:10).

I loved to cheerily quote to folks my favorite verse, "... God causes all thing to work together for good..."

However, I had neglected to read the next verses which further explain some of God's purposes:

"*And we know that God causes all things to work together for good to those who love God, to those who are called according to His purpose. For those whom He foreknew, He also predestined to become conformed to the image of His Son" (Romans 8:28–29).*

Ouch! God wants to press, squeeze, and mold me so that I am becoming more Christlike.

Only when the **Re**finer sees His own clear **re**flection on the surface of the melted gold is the process complete.

(Reference: "God's Refining Process" by June Hunt[29])

Chapter 18

FAITH*HOPE*LOVE

SOMETIMES, IT WAS so easy to focus on myself and my own problems that I lost sight of the fact that I was not the only person going through a season of trials and tribulations. In our small church, there was another tragedy that occurred in June of '87, two months before my rape in August. Sandy, a young mother in her early 30s, came home from aerobics, had some severe pain in her abdomen, and went to her doctor to check it out. He sent her over to the hospital for tests, and her husband, Michael, was at his desk at J.C. Penney, where he was a department manager, when the doctor called him with the shocking news, "Your wife is dying; you need to get here right away." Sandy had a rare liver condition called Bud-Chiari syndrome, an obstruction of the veins that carry blood out of the liver. She passed away exactly 30 days later.

Although I didn't know Sandy and Michael personally, I knew of them and had heard their inspiring testimony of how they had come to the Lord a few years before. It was hard to understand why the Lord took Sandy away so young, leaving behind her adopted son, Tanner, who was only eight months older than my son, Hudson. I directed them both in a Christmas piece that year, "Little Drummer Boy." Michael would be there to pick up his silly and rambunctious son from rehearsal, and I felt sad as I watched him talking to other men in the church, looking for some solace in his grief from the loss of his wife and the challenges of single parenting.

After the "key" incident, I came back from my secret fall retreat up north with the Mickelsons with some hope, encouraged and better able to meet my own set of circumstances as a single parent. The line of work I was in made it much easier for me to stay upbeat during my trials. I was blessed by the "exercise endorphins" that were released because of the high intensity aerobic classes I taught. It helped that the dance music of the '80s was, in my opinion, "awesome"! Also, I worked with children. Children = Energy + Enthusiasm + Creativity. It was always some form of fun, whether it was leading preschoolers in their locomotor skills or children in ballet, tap, and tumbling. The only drawback was the lack of financial stability that I so desperately needed. No worries; my Ms. Ann had an answer for that.

In December, I interviewed at a private Catholic school for a job as the physical education teacher ... teaching kindergarten through eighth grade co-ed. (i.e., that means middle school boys and girls together—yikes!!). Again, I had Ms. Masden to thank or hate for this opportunity. It was a crazy hard job, but I had a steady paycheck, and even though Dawn was not yet five years old, she was an intellectually "gifted child," so they let her join the kindergarten class (for free!) during my teaching hours of 8:00 a.m.–2:00 p.m. A big thank you again to my friend, **Re-** ... God's **grace** at work once more. At last, I had some temporary financial stability. (Do those words go together; temporary /stability?)

Even so, the men in our church kept me on their Saturday morning "work list." After the men's Saturday morning prayer breakfast, the guys would pile into pick-up trucks and do odd jobs and repairs for widows or other single women in need. My dryer went out, and one fateful Saturday morning in January, three men came over to fix it ... one of them being Michael, the young widower.

But the Greatest of These is Love

That was it ... that's how we officially met. That morning, God planted a tiny seed in each of our hearts, but we had no idea what would grow from those seeds:

> *"Though I do not believe that a plant will spring up where no seed has been, I have great faith in a seed ... convince me you have a seed there,*

And I am prepared to expect wonders"
(Henry David Thoreau).[30]

Spring is the time for young romantics to embrace and let their passion blossom into the full flower of love. After our winter seasons of sadness, Michael and I never expected to feel rejuvenated, like young kids again, full of hope for a happier future. Our courtship was rather unusual I guess by modern standards. We never went on an official date. Our families started sitting together at a table for Wednesday night potluck suppers. We shared a hymn book during service, with our kids on either side. We talked on the phone … a lot! We watched TV with the kids. We went to the high school track and ran. He came to rehearsals and my performance with the CENLA Ballet Theatre and sent me roses backstage. As the weather warmed, we joined in with all the families who would head out to the lake Sunday afternoons after service to picnic and go boating. We took a walk on the trail through the woods together, held hands, sat on a rock, and shared a kiss.

It was May, and we were gliding on the porch swing out in the backyard at Phyllis and Eddie's with all the kids running around playing tag. I think we both figured out it was a set-up, arranged by our matchmaker, Phyllis. Michael finally did pop "The Question," and everybody there went ballistic when we shared our good news. The kids were whooping it up, the brothers-to-be were wrestling in the yard, and the adults toasted with a glass of liqueur in a cordial celebration. All I could think of was God's goodness, and I remembered Paul Soileau's words to me almost a year ago as he patted me on my head inside his entryway and said, "Not all men are like this. God is going to bring you a good man someday."

Michael was that "good man." Just today—33 years later—I was looking for the Costco card in his drawer, and I found the small, folded note I had given him that May of '88. I had jotted down the adjectives that I thought described him then and still do today:

"I love you, and I find you witty & humorous; extremely caring, kind, and sensitive; charming; intelligent; full of grace & truth; godly; humble; handsome and very sexy."

That last part is why we decided to move our original wedding date up from October to July—we knew we couldn't wait that long and stay chaste to honor God in our physical relationship.

Which brings me to the sensitive subject—how does a sexual abuse and rape victim reconcile her past and move into a healthy sexual relationship?

Chapter 19

A WOMAN'S SACRED PLACE

BEFORE I REMARRIED, I had to "go deep" during my devotion times with the Lord to fully understand why the rape penetrated the most private and sacred part of my womanhood. I needed to heal and bring a sexual wholeness into the marriage with my new husband. In sharing these meditative thoughts, which I have further enhanced and developed through the years, I hope to bring insight and healing to other victims and perhaps give those in our life close to us a better understanding of our struggle to **re**cover and **re**build our life. As I said, these thoughts are "deep," but then so are the wounds that cut deep into the soul of a girl or woman who has been sexually abused or assaulted.

Re-, my friend, I need your soothing healing balm poured out on my female body and soul. I can't get through this on my own strength; I'm not even sure I can get past this attack at all. God, can you again give me your gift of sustaining **Grace**? Empower me with Your Holy Spirit as I pray:

"O Lord, You have searched me and known me . . .

For You formed my inward parts; You wove me in my mother's womb.

I will give thanks to You, for I am fearfully and wonderfully made; Wonderful are Your works, And my soul knows it very well"

(Psalm 139:1,13-14).

O God—You formed my inward female parts. You created me as a woman, in Your image.

Sexuality is sacred, part of my God-likeness.

My Sexuality is sacred and RAPE,

(I could also include unwanted sex, non-consensual sex, trafficked sex, paid sex, and child sexual abuse)

Is a VIOLATION of the innermost essence of my *Female Creation* . . .

That part of me created in the image of Almighty God.

It is a VIOLATION of God's design for perfect humanity:

Introduction

> *"God created man in His own image, in the image of God He created him; male and female He created them. God blessed them; and God said to them, be fruitful and multiply"* (Genesis 1: 27-28).

God first created the male, Adam, but declared that it was NOT good that Adam was alone . . .

Not good that the earth would be only a man's world, filled with male clones. God's design was incomplete.

God took a bone from Adam to create his soul mate, Eve … a BONE? Why Adam's rib? What's with the bone?

> *"So the Lord God caused a deep sleep to fall upon the man, and he slept; then He took one of his ribs and closed up the flesh at that place.*
>
> *The Lord God fashioned into a woman the rib which He had taken from the man, and brought her to the man.*
>
> *The man said,*
> *'This is now bone of my bones,*
> *And flesh of my flesh;*
> *She shall be called Woman,*
> *Because she was taken out of Man'"*
>
> (Genesis 2: 21-23).

Yes—there is some symbolism here:

God took Adam's rib to form the woman who would be his wife and life partner.

The rib is located under his arm for protection, and she would equally stand beside him in life.

The rib is also close to his heart to indicate the oneness they would share as "soul mates."

But specifically, a rib bone? God leaves out no details in designing His perfect creation.

The Lord God is the true "Father of Science."

It is known that the bone marrow—the spongy tissue found on the inside of the bone—is located primarily in the ribs. Within the marrow, the process of "hematopoiesis"—the production of blood cells takes place:

In the red bone marrow are formed:
- the red blood cells that carry oxygen to the body,
- the white blood cells that fight off infections, and
- the platelets, which help blood to clot and prevent uncontrolled bleeding.

In the yellow bone marrow:
- the fat is stored
- and it contains the mesenchymal STEM cells that can develop into bone, fat, cartilage, or muscle cells.[31]

Astounding!

Adam was created from the dust of the earth, from the basic elements.

But the woman, Eve, whose name in Hebrew comes from the word "to breathe" or "to live," was created from the warm, live bone marrow of the man, which can produce all the blood cells in the body:

> "... *the life of every creature is its blood*" (Leviticus 17:14).

Women Are All About Life:

- They bring LIFE into the world through childbirth.
- They breathe LIFE into others in their natural role as mothers, nurturers, teachers, and mentors.
- Like the STEM cells they were created from, they can adapt, grow, and develop in a myriad of ways.
- They are made from "bone." They are strong. They are the skeleton, the support, and the backbone of the family, of the church, of movements, organizations, and businesses.
- Pain is perceived at a deeper level in the bones. Nothing is more painful than a cancer that has metastasized to the bones.

My sacred feminine sexuality is the most special, private, unique part of God's design:

> *"For this reason a man shall leave his father and his mother, and be joined to his wife; and they shall become one flesh" (Genesis 2:24).*

The Lord God chose the earthly institution of marriage to illustrate our ultimate heavenly union with Christ. CHRIST is as the bridegroom and we, the church (individual believers), are as His beautiful bride:

As we symbolically walk down the aisle towards Christ Jesus, our waiting "bridegroom," He declares us innocent, holy, and blameless. We are His *virgin bride*.

Therefore:

When a man penetrates this innermost secret, sacred place in a woman (or girl)— against her will, without her permission, void of the loving relationship bonding them together—

There is irrevocable damage.

There is a tearing of the woman's sacred seal.

There is a herniation of her spiritual "hymen."

When her body is controlled against her will,

There is hurt and bruising in her human soul.

Rapists are robbers.

They steal not only a woman's body for a time, but the perpetrator attacks her very soul and wounds her spirit, forever leaving behind scars and a deep hole that seemingly cannot be filled or closed.

A woman who has been sexually assaulted experiences such inner turmoil that she wants to crawl into that dark hole and just disappear or escape to "the remotest part of the sea," a sea of sleep, or alcohol, drugs, chips, and chocolate. The tendency for her is to withdraw, isolate herself, and run away from everything and everyone ... including God:

> "Where can I go from Your spirit? Or where can I flee from Your presence?
>
> ... If I take the wings of the dawn, If I dwell in the remotest part of the sea,
>
> Even there Your hand will lead me, And Your right hand will lay hold of me.
>
> If I say, 'Surely the darkness will overwhelm me, And the light around me will be night,'
>
> Even the darkness is not dark to You, And the night is as bright as the day,

Darkness and light are alike to You" (Psalm 139:7–12).

God will not abandon me. He will pursue me. He will find me. In Him, I have lasting hope.

Time does heal some. Counseling helps some. Talking with other victims in support groups helps some.

My efforts took me so far, but the big breakthroughs were

unexpected gifts from God.

I have found that, at the deepest level, my healing has come through the holes in the hands of Jesus.

He knows what it is like to be wounded.

Jesus gets me!

He too had the visible scars of His suffering. Even in His resurrected body He carried the scars from the nails that were driven through His hands and feet on the cross and the sword that pierced His side.

> *"But Thomas, one of the twelve, called Didymus, was not with them when Jesus came. So the other disciples were saying to him, 'We have seen the Lord!' But he said to them, 'Unless I see in His hands the imprint of the nails and put my finger into the place of the nails, and put my hand into His side, I will not believe.' … Jesus came … and stood in their midst … Then He said to Thomas, 'Reach here with your finger, and see My hands; and reach here your hand and put it into My side; and do not be unbelieving, but believing.' Thomas answered and said to Him, 'My Lord and my God!'"*
>
> (John 20:24-25)

Jesus chose to keep the visible scars on His new, **re**surrected body. The wounds were not still open, red with inflammation, or oozing from infection. They were closed, healed up with new tissue and skin; only the indentations remained. Although

Jesus's body still carried a physical reminder of His suffering, there was no residual pain when Thomas put his fingers into those holes. There was a complete healing.

After the rape, I thought the wounds might never close, but healing has always been part of the ministry of Jesus, while on earth and now from heaven.

I have hope—I'm free: "*So if the Son makes you free, you will be free indeed*" (John 8:36).

I don't have to pretend that I'm "OK" and that the sexual assault and abuse never happened.

I do have emotional and spiritual scarring from that event that I will carry with me through this life.

This event, these scars, are part of "my story."

What I don't have anymore is the Guilt and Shame.

The child sexual abuse and the sexual assault are **NOT my fault!!!**

And it is NOT God's fault either. He is sad and grieved about sin.

It is the perpetrators and the rapist who sinned and used their free will to harm me.

They made me a victim, but I am an **innocent** victim.

Re- *and* Me

I honestly don't understand why God allowed this to be part of my story or anyone's story.

We live in a world bent towards evil with broken people who act on their evil desires.

What I do know is that God is still good and He promised that, "all things work together for good" (Romans 8:28). I believe that. God has showed me that is true. I trust Him. He loves me. He loves you.

Chapter 20

TRAUMA—DRAMA

PHYLLIS WAS MY matron of honor as well as the wedding planner, who unfortunately had only an eight-week window of time to work with before our July 23 date. She sewed matching pastel pink dresses for herself and our daughters, who would be the flower girls, and made their floral head wreaths and flower baskets. Hudson and Tanner would both be the ring bearers in their bow ties and suspenders. Phyllis coordinated our community of friends at church who wanted to "gift" us the whole wedding: REMARKABLE!

- Barry, who did the photo shoot for my F.U.N. brochures, was the wedding photographer.
- A lady who had a home-based cake baking business made the gorgeous three-tiered wedding cake.

- A "committee of church ladies" took on the flowers and decorations for the sanctuary.
- Another talented woman coordinated centerpieces, tablecloths, and table settings for the reception.
- Everyone brought fabulous homestyle southern and Cajun food for the brunch reception.
- A professional violinist, the mother of one of my ballet students, provided music for the ceremony.

PERFECT! Everything was arranged. In June, we made plans to drive with all three of our kids to meet each other's families—his in Waco and mine in Dallas. We were waiting in the car in front of my ex's rental house to pick up my children when a police car screeched up to the curb in front of us, and an officer jumped out.

We were told we could find you here. Your children have been in a terrible car accident!

Your son is already at Rapides General, and your daughter is being airlifted by helicopter.

You can follow us, and we will escort you there.

When it's sudden, when there are unknowns, when it is your children, no amount of praying can calm your racing heart and mind. My prayers were more like frantic pleas, begging God to be merciful, to take care of my children. I hung onto the arm rest as Michael sped through the streets following the squad car until we came to a dead **STOP**!

Right in front of the *railroad tracks* … remember the tracks that I said divided the town?

What kind of a backward town has railroad tracks blocking the only road to the hospital?!!!*@.

Finally, in the emergency room we were given the status of everyone; Hudson was being checked out but seemed to be OK except that his front teeth were knocked out. Dawn was unconscious in a coma—they were running scans. My ex's wife had been driving the car with her sister in the front seat, and the three children in the back seat, when they think she skidded off the slick road into the ditch and hit a tree. My ex's wife and her sister were in serious condition with multiple injuries, but her daughter was fine. Sharing a common concern over the well-being of your mutual children during a crisis has a way of giving perspective to custody battles.

This was the first time my ex and I were together in the same room talking, *without* our lawyers. We offered each other small gestures of reconciliation, and he gave me a brief reprieve from hostilities. We were both helpless, looking at our little girl, Dawn, as she lay motionless, not knowing if she would ever regain consciousness—and if she did, would there be brain damage?

It was a time for prayers, for peace, for **Grace**. **Re-** showed up in rare form, showering us with the Lord's lovingkindness, and all our prayers were answered positively. The next day,

Dawn came out of her coma and was released from the hospital with seemingly no repercussions, and my ex's new wife and sister-in-law also were able to go home later and heal up. Michael and I never did meet each other's families until the "Day of" ... but HEY! *The wedding was ON!*

I kept myself busy during the weeks before the wedding while my children were with their dad for his six-week summer visitation. I taught dance at another Summer Arts Break, this time down in Avoyelles Parish in the heart of Cajun country where many of the children only spoke a broken Cajun French; the Parisian French I spoke was only marginally helpful in trying to understand these adorable kids. The week before the big day, I went to the Cooper Aerobics Center in Dallas to certify as a Fitness Specialist (personal trainer).

So bizarre!! TRUTH is stranger than fiction.

I couldn't wait to get back to Alexandria and Michael, so when I reached the outskirts of town, I stopped at the gas station to use the pay phone to call him at work. When he answered and realized it was me, his voice dropped into a harsh hush as he directed me, "Don't dare go back to your house—don't let anyone see you! Be careful and go straight over to Pastor Bob and Sandy's, and pull your car around to the back, so it can't be seen from the street."

"Can you tell me what is going on?" I asked. "Not now, not time. I'll meet you there," he said.

My guard had been let down. The rapist's silent phone calls began to subside after the "key" incident in October and then had stopped altogether in January. The police were on the alert, looking for nighttime stalkers because he must have moved on to his next victim. He did, and he struck again in June with victim number five. Once more, he changed up his profile a bit: she was single, no children, and she did have a small dog. The rapist broke in undetected days before the rape, took her little barking dog, drove him way across town, and dropped him off. Not a very gentlemanly thing to do! The detectives had interviewed me again to see if they had missed any details that might lead them to this serial guy. I wondered if this had something to do with the rapist threatening me again.

When I got to the Vincents, I pulled around to the back and parked next to their travel trailer. I knocked on the kitchen door; they came out, and we climbed into the trailer to wait for Michael. Evidently, he knew the "hideout plan" because he came right up and tapped on the door of the trailer. What Bob and Sandy told us is so bizarre that I couldn't have made this all up if I had tried. The detectives at the APD were aware of all the help Jackson Street Church had given me after my attack and to victim number five, whose uncle was in our church. In fact, "good" rumors were being spread all over town about how incredibly loving and sacrificial the members of our church had been in supporting us through our traumas.

Pastor Bob had such a good reputation that when the detectives couldn't locate me, they called my pastor to find out where

I was! The detectives told Bob that the credible word out on the street is that someone was looking to hire a hit man to take me out before, or at, the wedding. Not only that, someone broke into my home while I was in Dallas, but it looked like all that was missing were some family photos and "personal" items pulled out of my vanity drawer—costume jewelry, scarves, etc. So then, did the police say who their person of interest was? Yes! They can't prove anything yet, but they believed it was Shelly, the babysitter for my children when they were at my ex's place. Shelly? Wow! The Vincents and I both have a long history with her from years back, and Bob has a theory for her motive:

The Vincents took Shelly in, to live with them, when she was a messed up single but pregnant young adult. Bob and Sandy helped arrange a private adoption, and I recall my husband and I visiting Shelly at the hospital right after her delivery; her baby was a girl, and I was pregnant with Dawn. We understood how hard it must be for her to give up her baby but assured her that her little girl was going to be raised in a loving and stable family. We lost contact with Shelly, but the next few years, she went back into the drug and criminal world and was shot in the stomach during an altercation in a lesbian bar. People in our church took her under their wing and were trying to help her again. My husband and I were asked to go visit her—to try and convince her to go straight and pull out of that seedy world. We offered Shelly the separate small apartment building behind our house, next to the garage, to live in, and ironically, I would "disciple" her. That is, to meet regularly to keep her on track, while I was the one off-track. In trying to be transparent about my own struggle with sin, I unwisely told Shelly about the guy at the health club. She was the whistleblower who alerted my husband and began the whole separation and divorce process. I guess I have her to "thank" for that because that was the final step to the ledge that brought me down, safely into the net of salvation by the **grace** of God, my friend, **Re-**.

To bring the "Shelly story" up to date ... she became my husband's chief live-in babysitter for my children during those crazy months immediately after the separation until I regained possession of my house right before that newscast of my "Nutcracker in a Nutshell" performance at the library. Shelly and her friends lived in my home for a time. I never saw what a disgusting mess it was in before I moved back because the ladies from the church went in to clean it up to spare me the shock. Phyllis described it to me much later: needles and drug paraphernalia strewn all over the den floor amid multiple sleeping bags and blankets. Full ashtrays with cigarette butts, empty food containers, empty alcohol bottles and dirty dishes in the kitchen and used feminine products thrown on the bathroom floor. Like I said, "disgusting."

By convenience and necessity, Shelly had remained as the children's chief babysitter for my ex through the years, getting ever more attached to my kids as "Aunt" Shelly, and this dangerous liaison is where Pastor Bob's theory comes to light. I guess Shelly had a lot to lose by me getting remarried to a nice, stable loving Christian man like Michael. Maybe if I remained a struggling single mom, the "anonymous coalition" could continue with their campaign of false child abuse cases and frivolous litigations attempting to influence a change of custody until I finally wore down and/or ran out of money for legal representation.

Bob had observed that Shelly had an unusual attachment to Dawn, and he conjectured that perhaps she could have transferred maternal emotions to my daughter who was born just a few months after the baby girl Shelly gave up at birth. The detectives agreed with his theory, and to add another layer of weirdness to the case, they were also investigating a voodoo cult she was said to be a part of that met in the deep piney woods for their rituals. They suspect that the reason why only "personal" items, not valuables, were stolen from my home is so that they could be used in a voodoo doll "death curse" against me. Indeed! **Truth is stranger than fiction!**

What now? To keep me safe the week before the wedding, Michael was to follow me over to Jack and Winnie Mertens (owner of Owl Grocery) who would hide my car in their garage and me in their spare upstairs bedroom. The detectives then came by to pick me up from their place and take me over to my house to pack up everything I would need for my wedding and honeymoon and to look to see what items specifically were missing from my vanity desk. That was it. The police dropped me back off at the Mertens for my pre-nuptial week of seclusion, and they assured me they would continue to search for leads as to the murder-for-hire plot but would also have several undercover cops at my wedding to keep a lookout for me.

I was accustomed to constant drama around me by now, and I witnessed how many times the Lord had "delivered me from evil," so even THIS didn't dampen my excitement in anticipation of my wedding day. Of course, Pastor Bob married us, and his marriage "message" to the congregation was more like a never-ending sermon, but with a great punchline. He chose as his illustration of all the trials Michael and I had gone through, the biblical account of Joseph and the Amazing Technicolor Dreamcoat: sold into slavery by his brothers, imprisoned, and freed to become second to pharaoh and savior to his family during the famine as he revealed who he really was.

> "As for you, you meant evil against me, but God meant it for good in order to bring about this present result . . ." (Genesis 50:20).

Finally, we were pronounced man and wife—celebrated with our friends and family at the reception, threw the bouquet, were showered with sachets of bird seed, and climbed into our decorated getaway car. After about 30 minutes of driving down the road towards New Orleans ecstatically laughing, kissing, reminiscing as only newlyweds can—I suddenly gasped. "What's wrong, what did you forget?" Michael asked.

"NOTHING! Oh my gosh!" I exclaimed. "I'm still alive! And we're married!"

Chapter 21

THE MIRACULOUS CALL

I WAS IN the middle of that frenetic time right before those greatly anticipated words are pronounced, "Dinner is ready!" I had eleven-month-old Stefan braced against my left hip as I stirred the sauce with my right hand and kept an eye on the pot of boiling spaghetti. Dawn was setting the table while Hudson was on the den floor playing with his two-year-old brother, Joffrey, when the phone rang. Dawn answered the call, "Mom, it's for you. It sounds long distance, but it's not Poppa or Mamoo."

"Oh," I said, a bit annoyed at the timing. "Then maybe it's one of the counselors from Tanner's camp."

"Hello, Rebecca. This is Chief Ritchie, and I have some good news for you," came a friendly and familiar voice that I recognized even without his introduction. I motioned to Dawn to take the baby into the den with his brothers as I turned off the pots on the stove and answered "Captain" Ritchie, who I had to remember was now "Chief" Ritchie, head of the Alexandria Police Department.

"Hi! OK. I'm ready—I hope it's the good news we have all been waiting to hear," I said with a tone of expectation in my voice.

"Yes!" Chief Ritchie affirmed. "We arrested the rapist yesterday in Georgia, extradited him here, and he is being held under bond."

"I just can't believe it," I exclaimed in relief, "even though you guys kept telling us you wouldn't quit until you caught him. Are you sure it's really him?"

"Absolutely, not a doubt; it's a perfect DNA match on you and victim number five as well. Ditto for the fingerprints he left on victim number five's bathroom windowsill, and we have other corroborating evidence that links him to your case and the first three. We have more than enough evidence for a conviction. Detective Cicardo did outstanding work nailing down this guy," bragged Chief Ritchie, rightly proud of his new captain of the detective unit.

"So, what are you able to tell me about the rapist," I asked him, "and how did he get up to Georgia?"

"His name is XXXX, he was married and lived in the same neighborhood as the first two victims. His wife divorced him, then he remarried and moved to a small town in Georgia," he told me and said that was all the information he could share with me for now.

"Married? That's surprising," I responded, rather astonished at this revelation.

"No, it didn't surprise us. Do you remember what Cicardo told you when he profiled our guy? This type of rapist is about power and control, and trust me, he is totally into the control thing," he revealed, giving me insight into the disturbed psyche of the criminal mind.

"Alright, you just let me know when the trial date is set because I am going to fly there and testify against him," I said with determination. "You know me well enough by now. I'm not going to back out and be afraid to face him. This jerk needs to be put away, so he can never hurt another woman."

"We're on the same page," Chief Ritchie agreed, "but this can get more complicated than you know."

Chief Ritchie finished up the conversation by giving me the run-down on all the "need to know." First the district attorney would be preparing the case for trial. As soon as the actual trial date was set, I would have to make plans for my family's care to be able to travel and stay until the trial concluded. There was no set timeline, so it could be a hardship for my family back home. I would be one of the chief witnesses against the defense. I had to be sure I could follow through.

I made a commitment to that end, and I thanked the chief and his staff for caring so much and never giving up the hunt for him these past seven years—from his first attack in 1985 until this fateful day of his capture in October of 1992. I hung up the phone, leaned up against the kitchen cabinet, and took that moment to turn away from the noise of the fun chaos of the kids playing behind me to gaze out to the picturesque view before me. There was a clear Florida sky with the evening sun reflecting off the water of our pool, surrounded by blooming flowers and grapefruit trees hanging over the fence. This was the moment I once had dreamt about, but did it really live up to my hype? Did that maybe ten-minute conversation with Chief Ritchie change my whole life in the way I thought it might? Not really.

The Miraculous Call

Not really? That's not very satisfying. Not really, but why? I believe that by God's **grace**, many years ago, **Re**-helped me **re**lease the rapist from having control over my future well-being; I forgave him for the harm, the hurt he had caused me. By forgiveness, I mean that I transferred my claims over to God because He alone is the one who judges and avenges all sin. I surrendered my "right" to bitterness and payback. I had already determined that my best way forward was to live my life and rob him of the satisfaction of breaking me. Long ago, I gave up hanging my life on this hoped-for "future moment," which I am now actually experiencing, to determine my present state of contentment. With that said, I did savor the moment and was **re**minded that God is just. We occasionally get a taste of

The Miraculous Call

His righteous condemnation on the evil in our world, which is just a foretaste of the complete justice He will deliver on the day of His final judgment on mankind.

At the time, I never knew exactly how the rapist was discovered and entrapped, but years later in 2005, when I had that hip replacement and thought back then that I would "write my book," I contacted the Alexandria Police Department to seek out Chief John Ritchie and Detective Tommy Cicardo. Chief Ritchie had retired and Detective Cicardo had been appointed the new police chief in 1997. He then retired himself and decided to write a book, *Because They Could*, about the policing, politics, slimy lawyering, and slanderous reporting that went on in Alexandria.

Alexandria was "Alemette," in his "fictional," but completely true account of that time period. This supposedly "fictional account" protected him from any libel lawsuits—but for those of us who know the true events and characters, the formula is simple … his fictional characters always had the exact same initials as their real-life counterparts: the real Tommy Cicardo was "Tony Caruso" and the real John Ritchie was "James Richards," etc. The real initials for the rapist are **R.D.H.**, and in his fictional book, he is Ronald David Hobard, but all the facts of the case are true. I must admit that I had some surreal moments when I read Tommy's book, getting all the inside scoop on me (unnamed victim number four) from the book, but most fascinating was the section entitled, "The Miraculous Call," which was the key to breaking the case.[32]

223

It's probably already clear that I personally don't buy into "coincidences;" in God's world—every seemingly unrelated random event is never out of His overarching control—part of His plan. If ever I had any doubts, God's engineering of the circumstances that led to the discovery and arrest of the serial rapist would have made me a believer. By the fall of 1992, Chief Ritchie and Detective Tommy Cicardo had explored all possible leads in the case of the "Uptown District Rapist," and the trail had grown cold with no more attacks since the last in 1988. It must have been a frustrating position to be in with the pressure from the public and the victims' families, both wanting closure and justice. The police had reached the limits of their human efforts, and then God stepped in with "the miraculous call," as they dubbed it. In relating what transpired, I am choosing to use the rapist's fictional name from Tommy's book.

The call came into the detectives' office from a Vivian Hobard, who requested an appointment in her home with Detective Cicardo and Chief Ritchie to help her through a problem she had in the past that involved the police department. When the officers came to her home, she invited them in and explained exactly why she asked for the meeting. She had been going through counseling because of her divorce and as part of her healing process, the psychologist said that she was to clear the air and tell the police about a lie she told them concerning the whereabouts of her son several years ago. She explained that when the police had come to her house inquiring about her son's location on certain dates, she knew he was out of town but lied about it. She and her son are rebuilding their relationship, so part of that process, according to her doctor, is for her to be truthful with her son and with the police. And oh, her doctor also insisted that she tell them about her controlling ex-husband, so they could understand her situation better. "*Mrs. Hobard had no idea, nor did they, where this conversation would lead,*" according to Thomas Cicardo's account in his book, the chapter titled, "Crimes of the Century."[33]

Their conversation went on for hours, with Vivian describing in detail some unusual stories about her ex she had never told anyone except her counselor—how he would take the fuse out of the dryer when he traveled, so no one could use it while he was gone, and she told them that he often left the house in the middle of the night and took Gaines Burgers with him, even though they didn't have a dog. She had seen a vibrator, women's panties, and other things that were not hers that he hid around the house and in his car. *(One of those "things" I'm sure was my nightgown—my attacker cut it off and took it with him as a "trophy.")*

By now, Chief Ritchie and Detective Cicardo suspected that her ex-husband, Ronald Hobard, could very well be the serial rapist. She continued answering all their questions as honestly as she could, and she even kept detailed records of their household. When Tommy asked her if Ronald, an accountant, ever traveled to San Antonio, she went upstairs and came down with a credit card receipt that Mr. Hobard had received in San Antonio. Tommy describes that moment this way in his book:

> "Tony" had read those files over and over. Although he had no notes with him, he quickly recognized the date on the receipt as being the same date the key was mailed back from San Antonio to victim four. "Rich" looked at him knowingly, and "Tony" nodded. They both knew then that Hobard was their man. The conversation continued, and they were able to fill in more blanks that tied Hobard to the crimes. Through the entire conversation, Vivian Hobard stayed focused on the purpose of the meeting, which was to tell the police of her ordeals with Ronald."[34]

"The purpose of the meeting … to tell the police of her ordeals with Ronald"? And just who set the agenda for that meeting? The good doctor! Imagine being Mrs. Hobard's psychologist, under strict confidentiality with the "counselor-client privilege" yet hearing information from Vivian that most certainly led him/her to believe that her ex-husband was the serial rapist. Without alarming or alerting Mrs. Hobart, her counselor devised a plan whereby he/she could use their influence to get Vivian to call the police to set up a meeting to talk about a small lie she told about her son to give them the bigger truths about her ex-husband and tip them off as to his real identity. The counselor helped set that in motion while keeping his/her integrity as a professional.

God "engineered" the circumstances and by His **grace**, **Re-** handed the police "their man" on a silver platter.

They worked closely with the district attorney's office to obtain all the necessary search warrants, but they did not tell another soul about the break in the case. They drove up to Georgia to the tiny town where Hobard lived with his beautiful, pregnant new wife and talked him into voluntarily giving a DNA sample and fingerprints to "eliminate" him as a suspect in another case they were working. When the DNA test results came back weeks later with a match, they drove back up with the search warrants and arrested him. That's when Chief Ritchie called me at our new home in Sarasota, Florida—where J.C. Penney had transferred Michael back in 1989, the year after we married.

The Injustice of Justice!

Justice doesn't always look like how you think it should. *Ronald David Hobard* was indicted on five counts of aggravated rape—each was a maximum of 30 years in state prison, and he had a fancy splashy lawyer to defend him. The case received so much pre-trial publicity that the trial had to be moved out of town, up to Shreveport. *Hobard's* "celebrity" lawyer cashed in on all the infamy that came with representing a "notorious" criminal. However, when he discovered the solid evidence against his client, he bailed on the case and another defender took over. All the other victims who still lived in Louisiana along with their angry husbands were ready to do their part to battle for justice and have their day in court. Unfortunately, we never got that day.

My plane ticket was on the kitchen counter, my bags were packed, and I was ready to fly out Sunday night when the phone rang that afternoon with another call from Chief Ritchie. There would be no trial.

A plea bargain was made and accepted behind closed doors. Chief Ritchie explained the details to me and said even though it didn't feel like the big WIN we all wanted, the rapist was still going to prison and would be locked up for quite a while. He said that these cases can be tricky, DNA evidence is new to the court system, and many things can go wrong to get a mistrial or no conviction at all, so the rapist's defense attorney took the plea offer presented by the district attorney. At the time, I was infuriated, feeling like the DA's office took the cowardly back door and robbed all of us of our front and center, "day in court." However, a better understanding of all the factors in play shed light on the process involved in making difficult legal decisions.

It turns out that Louisiana at the time had some strange, and I would even say "unfair," laws for setting punishments and dealing with criminal convictions of rape. The law stated that aggravated rape with a deadly weapon was a max of 30 years, BUT forcible rape without a deadly weapon was only seven years! The defense revealed their strategy: they claimed the switchblade *Hobard* used on us during the rapes was not used as a weapon, but only as a "tool" for cutting clothes, ropes, and tape. You could have fooled me!

It sure FELT like a weapon up against my throat before clothes and ropes were cut. I knew he had a knife during the assault. I never knew what he might do to stab me, to kill my children.

Nevertheless, the agreement was two fifteen-year sentences for the assaults with DNA and fingerprint evidence—my case, number four, and number five, and nine of those years would be without any chance for parole. He wouldn't get paroled ever if we had our way because all five of us would be writing letters to the parole board petitioning them to keep him in prison. What we didn't count on was a disaster called "Katrina."

When Hurricane Katrina hit New Orleans in August of 2005, it caused major flooding and disruption in the state penal system with loss of prison space for convicted criminals. There simply was not enough space left in the state of Louisiana to hold all the prisoners. There was no time/money to build more prisons, so they needed to have less prisoners. Their solution? The state could not overturn each individual case and change the sentencing, but what they did do was pass a new law to take an entire classification of the prison population that met certain criteria and cut their prison sentence in half! Our guy had served part of his 30 years and passed the nine years without parole mark, so he was released after serving half of his sentence, only 15 years.

I received a nice letter from the prison warden when he was released. I got another letter when he violated parole and was sent back to prison and a third letter when he was released again. I've never made any attempt to contact or visit my attacker, but Chief Ritchie and Detective Circardo did, to follow up on some of the details of their profile of him for their records and to see if he was responsible for any other cases they might have missed. One of the pieces of information they wanted from him was how he selected his victims.

For me, he told them that he saw me coming out of Jack Merten's Owl Grocery store on a Sunday afternoon dressed from church and thought I "looked good, and so he followed me home to my nearby duplex." He then kept following me and the children for a year after I moved back into my home in the Garden District.[35]

When *Hobard* came into the interview room at the prison, they said he brought a Bible in with him. First, he talked with the Alexandria police officers about "religion" and told them he had found Jesus. They said they patiently heard him out, but Tommy was skeptical. To the "I found Jesus" story, he popped back with the classic line, "Jesus was never lost."[36]

I'm probably not as doubtful, and I sincerely hope that it's true. I am more optimistic because I had the rewarding experience of participating in the prison ministry branch of "Evangelism Explosion" with Art Hallett Ministries. For two years I traveled with Art and his group of volunteers through the Florida State and Georgia Federal prison systems—speaking and giving dance performances to the prison populations there … both men and women. I witnessed many genuine transformations as prisoners heard the Gospel message and dedicated their lives to following Jesus.

God's Word is powerful and can reach into any sinner's heart. I had already dealt with forgiving the rapist for what he did to me and my children, and he was held accountable, sent to prison, and punished for his crimes. If he did sincerely **re**pent of his actions and sinful life by the gift of God's **grace**, then he too would be **re**born into a new life.

Re-and Me
Life NOW with My Little 2-Letter Friend

"**Re-**" or rather, **grace**, is amazing. If she was the means by which a wretch like me found Jesus on the couch in Conroe so I could begin the lifelong journey of becoming **Re**-Becky, a new creature in Christ, then NO ONE is beyond being forgiven and **re**stored to a **re**lationship with our Heavenly Father. Not only was she my saving **grace**, but she has never left my side, consistently providing me with a supernatural sustaining **grace** at the moment I needed her help. She **re**minds me daily from these verses in (I Thessalonians 5:16-18) to:

> "**Re**joice always; pray without ceasing; in everything give thanks for this is God's will for you in Christ Jesus."

YES! KNOW THAT THERE IS HOPE!

Remember that you can handle whatever
is thrown at you in life because . . .

"The WILL of God Won't Lead You Where the GRACE of God Can't Keep You."

And Oh Yeah … God is Everywhere!

Acknowledgments

I AM IMMENSELY GRATEFUL for discovering My Word Publishing through a friend of mine who lives in Denver and attended a book launch for an author who successfully self-published using their services. From my first consultation with owner, Polly Letofsky, I knew that she was shooting it to me straight as a person who had learned the hard way the frustrating and expensive pitfalls of publishing your own book. That experience inspired her to develop her own company with a mission "to assure authors get through the self-publishing of their book seamlessly, swiftly, and affordably". She has not failed to give me the correct advice and allowed me to pick and choose those services I truly needed from the incredibly talented team of professionals she has gathered around her.

I am indebted to my most wise and wonderful My Word Publishing book consultant, Kirsten "Kiki" Ringer who guided me through the entire process with her insightful suggestions and patiently kept me moving forward. Our Zoomie time together was always fun, creative, and productive. Victoria Wolf of Wolf Design and Marketing is a graphic artist of immense talent who took my clumsy conceptions and transformed them into beautiful art. Her book cover and layout designs exceeded my expectations. And my goodness, how I appreciate the thorough work of my proof editor, Laura Dent, The Durango Wordsmith, who patiently taught me the tools I would need to review her edit. As a person with "some" English teaching background, I figured she would find only a "few" grammatical, punctuation, and formatting errors to correct in my script…boy, was I humbled and thankful for her keen eye.

Getting a book project completed and "off to print" is only half of what needs to be done to get it to the reader. Again, Polly came through with her current area of expertise: Self Marketing in today's world of evolving social media opportunities as described in her *BUZZ! Your Super Sticky Book Marketing Plan*. I will forever be trying to adapt to the "new" ways of social media promotion.

If you ever considered authoring a book of any genre, I wouldn't hesitate to recommend Polly Letofsky and her team with My Word Publishing. Authoring a book was not at all as "romantic" as I had imagined it, in fact it was tedious and emotionally frustrating, but with the help of this outstanding team it did become a reality and I am glad I was able to persevere and learn so much from them!

About the Author

REBECCA BURNETT SWIECZKOWSKI has taught and coached dance, fitness, or physical education at every educational level. She has a passion to encourage and inspire her students as well as support those who especially struggle with life's challenges. Rebecca draws on her faith in God who has given her a renewed purpose through the many opportunities and learning experiences she has had as a wife, mother to her five children, professional ballet dancer, and business owner. Rebecca lives in Frisco, Texas, and loves to spend time with her husband, Michael, and their chihuahua, Cupcake—biking, hiking, and gardening when she is not training clients in her Get ReFormed Pilates studio.

January 1987: Dawn, Rebecca, and Hudson.

November 1991: From bottom, Joffrey, Hudson, Dawn with baby Stefan, and Tanner.

December 1988: Left to Right, Hudson, Rebecca, Dawn, Tanner and Michael

Endnotes

1 "40 Courageous Quotes from Evangelist Billy Graham," Debbie McDaniel, http://www.crosswalk.com/faith/spirituallife/inspiring quotes.

2 Tony Evans, *The Grace of God* (Chicago, IL.: Moody Publishers,2004), 20.

3 Dr. Bob Ward and Mac Engel, *Building The Perfect Star* (Olathe, KS.: Ascend Books, 2015), Book Jacket.

4 Ibid., 12.

5 Ibid., Book Jacket

6 Ibid., Endorsements

7 Kavitha A. Davidson, "A look at the untold story of the Dallas Cowboys cheerleaders", http://www.espn.com/espnw/cultural, (March 16, 2018).

8 "Space Shuttle *Challenger* Disaster", http://www.wikipedia.org/wiki/space_shutle_challenger_disaster.

9 *"Steel Magnolias",* http://www.wikipedia.org/wiki/Steel_Magnolias.

10 Oswald Chambers, *My Utmost for His Highest* (Grand Rapids, MI.:Discovery House Publishers,1992), January 1.

11 Angela Wendell Hayes, *"F.U.N. aerobics combines methods", The Town Talk, Alexandria-Pineville, La,* August 16,1987.

12 *DNA Technology in Forensic Science: Summary,* http://www.ncbi.nlm.nih.gov.>books>NBK234547.

13 Statement on Emergency Contraceptive in Cases of Rape, Catholic Medical Association, http://www.ncbi.nlm.nih.gov.books.NBK234547.

14 *Woman raped by intruder in home, The Town Talk, Alexandria-Pineville, LA.,*August 19,1987.

15 Dr. Jim Denison, *An Honest Approach to the Mystery of Suffering,* http://www.jimdenisonlibrary.org/tag/suffering, July 29,2018.

16 Greenville, Texas. http://www.wikipedia.org/wiki/Greenville_Texas#:~:text=Greenville. July 7, 1921.

17 Jerry Humpries, *"'Gentleman rapist' sought in 4 rapes", The Town Talk,* December 30, 1987.

18 Evander Holyfield vs Mike Tyson II., https://en.wikipedia.org/wiki/Evander_Holyfield_vs._Mike_Tyson_II.

19 Ibid., 37.

Endnotes

20 *Testimony,* https://www.meriam-webster.com/dictionary/testimony

21 *Evangelism,* https://www.etymonline.com/word/evangelism

22 *Evangelical,* https://www.meriam-webster.com/dictionary/evangelical

23 Oswald Chambers, *My Utmost for His Highest* (Grand Rapids, MI.: Discovery House Publishers, 1992), October 5.

24 Rebekah, www.abarim-publications.com/meaning/Rebekah

25 Robbi Zacharias, https://www.goodreads.com/author/quotes/6977444.R_Zaharias

26 Henri Nouwen, *I love you, I love you, I love you,* https://www.denisonforum.org/columns/daily-article/a-church-employs-the-unemployed-to-feed-those-in-need-two-responses-to-our-fear-of-inadequacy. March 26, 2020.

27 Ibid.,

28 Elisabeth Elliot, *Through Gates of Splendor* (Lincoln, NE.: Tyndale House Publishers, Inc., 2005), 263-267.

29 June Hunt, *God's Refining Process,* http://www.hopefortheheart.org.march-2015-gods-refining-process/.

30 Henry David Thoreau, *Though I do not believe that a plant,* https://www.goodreads.com/quotes/50844-though-i-do-not-believe-that-a-plant-will-spring.

31 Bone Marrow, https://en.wikipedia.org/wiki/Bone_marrow.

32 Thomas Cicardo, *Because They Could* (Alexandria, LA.: Red River X-Press, 2005),

33 Ibid., 77.

34 Ibid., 78

35 Ibid., 44.

36 Ibid., 86

Made in the USA
Columbia, SC
30 March 2025